THE WAY OF TRUTH IN A WORLD OF FICTION

Beyond *The Da Vinci Code*

From the Bible-Teaching Ministry of

CHARLES R. SWINDOLL

INSIGHT FOR LIVING

THE WAY OF TRUTH IN A WORLD OF FICTION

Beyond The Da Vinci Code *Workbook*

Charles R. Swindoll has devoted his life to the clear, practical teaching and application of God's Word and His grace. Chuck currently is the senior pastor of Stonebriar Community Church in Frisco, Texas; but his listening audience extends far beyond this local church body. As a leading program in Christian broadcasting, *Insight for Living* airs in major Christian radio markets around the world, reaching people groups in languages they can understand. Chuck's extensive writing ministry has also served the body of Christ worldwide and his leadership as president and now chancellor of Dallas Theological Seminary has helped prepare and equip a new generation for ministry.

Based upon the original outlines, charts, and transcripts of Charles R. Swindoll's sermons, the workbook text was developed and written by Michael J. Svigel, Th.M., Ph.D. candidate, Dallas Theological Seminary, a creative writer in the Creative Ministries Department of Insight for Living.

Editor in Chief: Cynthia Swindoll, President, Insight for Living

Vice President: Wayne Stiles, Th.M., D.Min., Dallas Theological Seminary
Theological Editors: Marla Alupoaicei, Th.M., Dallas Theological Seminary
Greg Smith, M.A., Biblical Studies, Dallas Theological Seminary
Content Editors: Brie Engeler, B.A., University Scholars, Baylor University
Amy Snedaker, B.A., English, Rhodes College
Copy Editor: Jim Craft, M.A., English, Mississippi College
Proofreaders: Melissa Carlisle, M.A., Christian Education, Dallas Theological Seminary
Mike Penn, B.A., Journalism, University of Oklahoma
Cover Designer: Tony Muelle, A.A.S., Oklahoma City Community College
Production Artist: Nancy Gallaher, B.F.A., Advertising Art, University of North Texas
Cover Image: Superstock, Inc.

Published by IFL Publishing House, A Division of Insight for Living
Post Office Box 251007, Plano, Texas 75025-1007

Printed in the United States of America
ISBN: 1-57972-697-6

Table of Contents

A Letter from Chuck

Dear Friend:

Don't get me wrong, I like a good book or film—a well-spun tale that not only entertains, but also informs and inspires. But Hollywood can go too far . . . and often does. Sometimes a work of fiction treads arrogantly on holy ground—blaspheming the most fundamental truths about the person and work of Jesus Christ. *The Da Vinci Code*—like *The Last Temptation of Christ* years ago—is one such work that I believe has taken that presumptuous step across the line.

The problem with this type of fiction is that it sounds plausible to many uninformed and undiscerning people. We've heard stories of unbelievers being turned away from the faith and weak believers becoming confused with doubts. And it doesn't help that Ivy League scholars show up on our television screens with evidence supporting some of the history of these novels and films.

Although *The Da Vinci Code* is only a work of fiction and its outrageous claims about Christianity can easily be refuted, other more important questions instantly rise to the surface:

- Where did our Bible come from?
- Are there really "lost Scriptures" that support a "lost Christianity"?
- How can I be sure that Jesus was God and that He died and rose again?
- Where do we draw the line between orthodoxy and heresy in our age of diversity?

These and other questions lie behind the fiction of *The Da Vinci Code* and the relentless attacks by unbelieving scholars on the historical Christian faith. That's why we put together several key lessons touching on these critical issues.

It's my sincere hope that the lessons in this workbook will not only make you aware of the crucial issues of the current conflict and strengthen your own faith but also equip you to gently engage both the misled and the misleading. In short—to point out the way of truth in a world of fiction.

Charles R. Swindoll

How to Use This Workbook

The 2003 novel, *The Da Vinci Code*, stirred up a great deal of controversy concerning the origins of Christianity and the Bible. However, Dan Brown's work of fiction represents merely a small twig on a larger tree of criticisms that strike at the foundations of the faith. Other branches of this same tree include the Jesus Seminar, the quests for the "historical Jesus," the false Christs of the cults, and the well-publicized criticisms of historians seen frequently on television and in magazines.

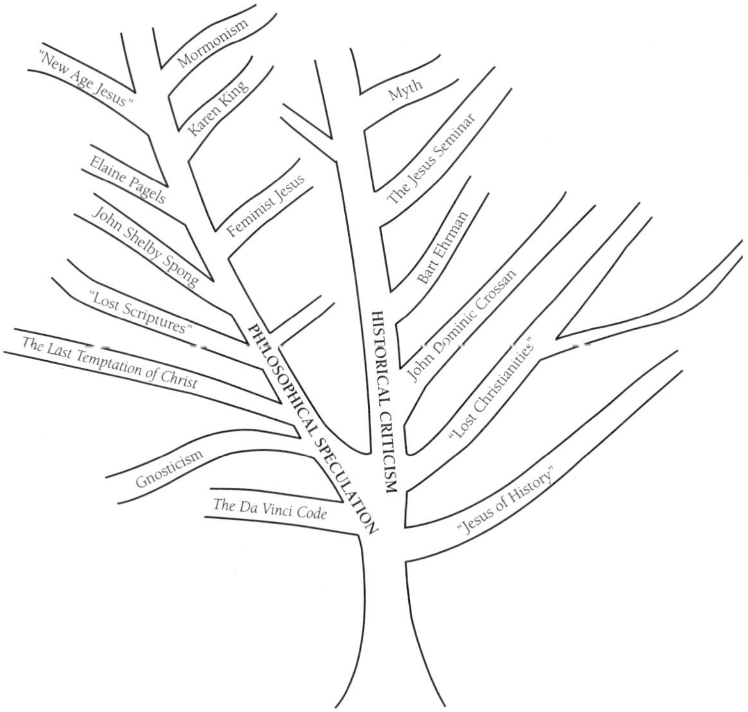

The roots of this tree run much deeper than the far-out fiction of *The Da Vinci Code*, delving into some deeper questions that this workbook will begin to answer, such as:

- Where do we draw the line between accepted Christian truths and falsehoods?
- Where did heretical writings come from?
- How did we get the set of Scriptures that make up our modern Bible?
- Can the Bible be trusted?
- What did the earliest Christians believe about Jesus?
- How did the early church grow and develop?
- Who were the founders of the early church, and why are they important?

The outrageous claims of *The Da Vinci Code* have already been addressed in several excellent resources (see "Resources for Probing Further" in the back of this workbook). However, this workbook is designed to introduce you to the deeper issues that historians, scholars, and theologians are talking about. You'll see these debates in newspapers and magazines, as well as on public television and prime-time specials . . . issues that go way beyond *The Da Vinci Code*.

The Way of Truth in a World of Fiction: Beyond The Da Vinci Code *Workbook* will strengthen your confidence in the foundations of the Christian faith and begin to equip you to take a stand in an increasingly anti-Christian world. At the same time, you'll explore in a practical way the classic doctrines of the Christian faith—especially the truth concerning Scripture and Jesus Christ.

A brief introduction to the overall structure of each lesson will help you get the most out of these studies, whether working individually or as part of a group.

Lesson Organization

Each of the thirteen lessons begins with **THE HEART OF THE MATTER**, which highlights the main idea of the lesson for rapid orientation. The lesson itself is then composed of three main teaching sections—"You Are Here," "Discovering the Way," and "Starting Your Journey."

YOU ARE HERE includes an introduction and thought-provoking questions to orient you to the topic that will be examined in the lesson. Groups should plan to spend ten to fifteen minutes in this section.

DISCOVERING THE WAY explores the principles of Scripture through observation and interpretation of key Bible passages, demonstrating the relevance of the Bible to answer critics both ancient and modern. Parallel passages and additional questions supplement the key Scriptures for more in-depth study. This section should require twenty to thirty minutes of group time.

STARTING YOUR JOURNEY focuses on specific, activity-oriented applications to help you put into practice the principles of the lesson in ways that fit your personality, gifts, and level of spiritual maturity. Since no single book or Bible study could delve exhaustively into all the relevant historical, biblical, and theological issues, we've compiled a list of resources in the back of this workbook to help you probe further and grow deeper in these matters. A group should cover this section in about ten to fifteen minutes.

In the workbook's expanded margins, you'll find plenty of space for taking notes, as well as insightful quotations and useful Leader Helps containing suggestions for working in a group setting.

Using the Workbook for Small-Group Study

Designed with the small group in mind, *The Way of Truth in a World of Fiction: Beyond* The Da Vinci Code *Workbook* will be most effective when studied by two or more people with a facilitator. The following suggestions are recommended if you're serving as the small-group facilitator.

Preparation. All group members should try to prepare in advance by working through the lessons as described later under "Using the Workbook for Individual Study." As the leader, you should take additional steps to supplement your preparation either by listening to the corresponding sermons (available for purchase at **www.insight.org**) or by reading any of the recommended resources. Mastery of the material will build your confidence and competence, and approaching the topic from various perspectives will equip you to freely guide discussion.

Discussion Questions. You should feel free to mold the lesson according to the needs of your unique group. At a minimum, however, the group should cover the questions marked by the group icons in each of the three main sections during your meeting time. While planning the lesson, you will want to mark additional questions you feel fit the time allotment, needs, and interests of the group. The questions are divided to assist you in your lesson preparation. Note that the question series marked by the clock icon are *primary*—meant to contribute to a solid understanding of the lesson. The unmarked question series is *secondary*—intended to provide a deeper exploration of the topic and corresponding Scripture passages. Encourage your group members to dig into these questions on their own.

Flexibility. During group time, after opening in prayer, lead the group through the lesson you planned in advance. Members may want to share their own answers to the questions, contribute their insights, or steer the discussion in a particular direction that fits the needs of the group. Sometimes group members will want to discuss questions you may have left out of the planned lesson. *Be flexible*, but try to stay on schedule so the group has sufficient time for the final section, "Starting Your Journey," where the application of the lesson begins.

Goal. If it's unrealistic to complete a single lesson during a session, consider continuing where you left off in the next session. The goal is not merely to cover material but to promote in-depth, personal discussion of the topic with a view toward personal response and application. To do this, the group will need to both understand the biblical principles and apply them to their lives.

Using the Workbook for Individual Study

The Way of Truth in a World of Fiction: Beyond The Da Vinci Code *Workbook* may also be used for individual study. Here's the method we recommend:

Prayer. Begin each lesson with prayer, asking God to teach you through His Word and to open your heart to the self-discovery afforded by the questions and text of the workbook.

Scripture. Have your Bible handy. We recommend the New American Standard Bible or another literal translation, rather than a paraphrase. As you progress through each workbook lesson, you'll be prompted to read relevant sections of Scripture and answer questions related to the topic. You will also want to look up Scripture passages noted in parentheses.

Questions. As you encounter the workbook questions, approach them wisely and creatively. Not every question will be applicable to every person all the time. If you can't answer a question, continue on in the lesson. Use the questions as general guides in your thinking rather than rigid forms to complete. If there are things you just don't understand or that you want to explore further, use the wide margins to jot down your thoughts or questions.

Features. Throughout the chapters, you'll find several special features designed to add insight or depth to your study. Use these features to enhance your study and deepen your knowledge of Scripture, history, and theology. An explanation of each feature can be found beginning on the next page.

Our prayer is that the biblical principles, exercises, and applications in this workbook will help you not only discern the way of truth in a world of fiction but also grow deeper in the Christian life.

Special Workbook Features

Lessons are supplemented with a variety of special features to summarize and clarify teaching points or to provide opportunities for more advanced study. Although they are not essential for understanding and applying the principles in the lesson, they will offer valuable nuggets of insight as you work through this material.

GETTING TO THE ROOT

While our English versions of the Scriptures are reliable, studying the original languages can often bring to light nuances of the text that are sometimes missed in translation. This feature explores the meaning of the underlying Hebrew or Greek words or phrases in a particular passage, sometimes providing parallel examples to illuminate the meaning of the inspired text.

DIGGING DEEPER

Various passages in Scripture touch on deeper theological questions or confront modern worldviews and philosophies that conflict with a biblical worldview. This feature will help you gain deeper insight into specific theological issues related to the biblical text.

DOORWAY TO HISTORY

Some knowledge of history is vital to addressing the issues brought up by today's critics of the Christian faith. Therefore, this feature takes you back in time to explore the personalities, literature, and events of the early years of the church—that formative period of history often twisted by unbelieving scholars. In the workbook margins, you'll find inspiring and insightful quotations from early church fathers. Mentored and taught by the New Testament apostles themselves, these believers took a bold stand for truth.

TRUTH OR FICTION?

Some of the strange ideas in fictional works like *The Da Vinci Code* and even in books claiming to present the "true" history of early Christianity can be refuted with just a few simple facts. This feature provides you with quick answers to some of these outrageous claims.

THE WAY OF TRUTH IN A WORLD OF FICTION

Beyond *The Da Vinci Code*

Lesson One

An Exposé of Counterfeit Communicators

2 Peter 2:1–3

THE HEART OF THE MATTER

Beware . . . can you recognize a counterfeit? Whether it is art or money, products or publications, phonies have pushed their wares on the unwary since the beginning of creation. Any fraudulent sham is harmful, but none are more devastating than false prophets and phony teachers who present their lies as religious or historical truth. The Bible reserves some of its severest words for those who act as though they speak and live the truth but are, in fact, false in word and deed.

YOU ARE HERE

We have all been victimized by a con artist at one time or another. It happens—more often than we'd like to admit. Perhaps you've been bamboozled by a forgery or a bogus investment scam. Maybe you only lost your spare change; maybe you lost your life savings. Or perhaps it nearly cost you your sanity, as Christopher Edwards experienced. In the foreword

Leader Help

By the end of this lesson, group members should be aware of the serious problem of heresy and its modern deceptive forms; and they should be moved to strengthen their own knowledge of the truth, to engage in spiritual battle against heresy, and to guard others from deception.

of his book, *Crazy for God,* he recounts part of his personal nightmare:

> My story began innocently enough when I was lured into a "fun" weekend in June of 1975 on a farm owned by a front group for Sun Myung Moon's Unification Church. . . .
>
> . . . I was transformed from an intelligent, independent human being into a completely subservient disciple of my new Messiah—terrified of questioning, dependent on my leaders for my every move, ready and willing to die or even kill to restore the world under the absolute rule of Reverend Moon.[1]

Leader Help
If any group members have experienced religious deception by a cult or false teacher, ask if they would be willing to share it. If not, move to a discussion of the following questions.

Recall a time when you were "ripped off"—not just robbed of your material possessions but personally cheated. How did you feel about the person who tricked you? How did you feel about yourself? Consider the following arenas of life to help you remember.

Finances

Relationships

Spiritual/Religious Life

Education

Workplace

Looking back, could you have avoided or prevented the deception? What might you have done? What actions might you have taken?

____

____

____

____

____

How does this experience affect your level of trust when you encounter similar situations?

____

____

____

____

____

DISCOVERING THE WAY

Of all the cons to which we might fall prey, the most damaging is the deception of a religious phony. Swindlers of this kind deal in counterfeit truth, an imitation meant to fool the unsuspecting. Every day peddlers of falsehood receive nodding approval on television, in bookstores, on the silver screen . . . and even behind pulpits. Counterfeit truth is big business, and it is still owned and operated by the same insidious proprietor who started it millennia ago . . . in a garden (Genesis 3).

The Original Counterfeit

In 2 Corinthians 11:3, Paul wrote about the world's first con artist, his methods, and his goal: "But I am afraid that, as the serpent deceived Eve by his craftiness, your minds will be led astray from the simplicity and purity of devotion to Christ." This "serpent," of course, is Satan, whom Jesus described as one who "does not stand in the truth because there is no truth in him. Whenever he speaks a lie, he speaks from his own nature, for he is a liar and the father of lies" (John 8:44). How does Satan work? What does he do to spread his counterfeit "truth" throughout the world?

First of all, Satan is in the deception business. He commits himself wholeheartedly to his operation. He opened up his shop by selling Eve a bite of deception through his masterful craftiness. He's the father of lies, and he intentionally seeks to know his victims' weaknesses so he can exploit them, just as he did with Eve.

Second, Satan targets the mind. He knows that once the mind has been duped into believing a lie, the heart, will, and emotions quickly follow. What is Satan's ultimate goal? He desires to lead people away "from the simplicity and purity of devotion to Christ" (2 Corinthians 11:3).

Third, Satan "disguises himself as an angel of light" (2 Corinthians 11:14) and subtly substitutes his lies for God's truth. With his power of deception, Satan can make the most obvious lies seem as if they were gloriously inspired, well-founded on historical or scientific facts, and worthy of our belief and trust.

"Be wary of false preachers who smile a lot, dripping with practiced sincerity. Chances are they are out to rip you off some way or other. Don't be impressed with charisma; look for character. Who preachers are is the main thing, not what they say. A genuine leader will never exploit your emotions or your pocketbook. These diseased trees with their bad apples are going to be chopped down and burned."
(Matthew 7:15–20 MSG)

> Error, indeed, is never set forth in its naked deformity, lest, being thus exposed, it should at once be detected. But it is craftily decked out in an attractive dress, so as, by its outward form, to make it appear to the inexperienced (ridiculous as the expression may seem) more true than the truth itself.[2]
>
> —Irenaeus of Lyons (c. AD 185)

Fourth, Satan uses various people to accomplish his goals, and they "disguise themselves as servants of righteousness" (2 Corinthians 11:15). Like their master, these servants of deception will seem doctrinally sound, historically plausible, intelligent, caring, and worthy of support. But what they are actually offering is a false righteousness, a false Messiah, a false hope, and a false knowledge.

Recall the personal experience of deception you identified at the beginning of this lesson. Did any of these four methods of deception find their way into your story as well? If so, explain how.

Today Satan has more means of deception at his disposal than ever before. Television, film, video games, the Internet—all of these are able to spread lies more effectively, more swiftly, and to more people than any methods of the past. When you add in radio, books, newspapers, magazines, and everyday conversation, the opportunities for deception seem endless.

Why do you think that electronic forms of media are especially persuasive means of spreading lies? What traits or characteristics make them particularly convincing?

How are Satan's four modes of deception (described on pages 5 and 6) reflected in the various means of deception available today? Give specific examples.

Which means of deception are you most susceptible to, especially in subtle ways? Why do you think these are difficult for you?

DOORWAY TO HISTORY
Historic Heresies

Jesus and the apostles predicted the coming of false prophets and teachers who would deceive unprepared Christians and rob unbelievers of the truth (Matthew 24:11; 2 Peter 2:1). Although they differed from one another in many ways, each of these heretics rejected the central truths of the Christian faith. Consider a few of the most ancient heretics and their modern counterparts.

Cerinthus (c. AD 100) denied the true incarnation of Christ, teaching that Christ was only a spiritual being who adopted the body of the man, Jesus. The apostle John may have written the fourth gospel directly against Cerinthus's heresy. Today some teach that the "Christ of faith" is just an ideal, mythical figure we should strive to imitate rather than the real, incarnate God-man.

Gnostics (c. AD 100–200) taught that Christ was only one of many spirit beings that sprang forth from God to bring salvation by special knowledge (*gnosis*) only to the spiritually elite. They wrote their own scriptures to support their views. Gnostic elements are currently found in New Age mysticism, extreme charismatic groups, and Mormonism. The Gnostic "gospels" have also become increasingly popular.

Ebionites (c. AD 100–150) were Jewish Christians who emphasized the observance of the law and denied the virgin birth and deity of Christ. Many modern critical historians, such as members of the Jesus Seminar, emphasize the "historical Jesus"—teaching that Jesus was a good moral teacher but not the Son of God.

Marcion (c. AD 150) completely rejected the Old Testament and accepted only a few New Testament books after editing them to fit his theology of two opposing gods and an evil material universe. Similarly, many of today's critical scholars reject most books of the Bible as forgeries and suggest the Bible has several competing theologies rather than the unifying theme of the one triune God.

Arius (c. AD 320) denied the true deity of Christ and taught that the Son had a beginning. Therefore, Jesus was a created being. After promoting his heresy with delightful ditties that caught the attention of the common people, Arius's teachings were condemned at the Council of Nicaea. Jehovah's Witnesses hold similar heretical views about Jesus Christ.

A Portrait of False Teachers

The apostle Peter vigorously warned against people who peddle false teaching. The first three verses of 2 Peter 2 provide us with a classic description of these deceivers.

Read 2 Peter 2:1–3. As you read, note at least ten observations about the false teachers' characteristics or actions. You may either circle them in your Bible or jot them down here:

____

____

____

____

____

Peter summarized several different ways in which counterfeit communicators operate. First, counterfeit communicators deceitfully present heresy as truth (2 Peter 2:1). Most often, they do not blatantly deny the truth in the beginning. Instead, they offer up their poison in a mixture of sweet nectar to coax us into what we think is just a harmless sip. They want us to choose between their alluring teaching and that of orthodox Christianity, so they dress up their views in the garb of plausibility—even respectability.

GETTING TO THE ROOT

The term "heresy" (as used in 2 Peter 2:1) comes from the Greek word *haireseis*. The method used for introducing falsehood is revealed in the word *heresy*. In Greek it conveys the idea of "making a choice."[3] Counterfeit communicators are masters of what Peter called "false words" in 2 Peter 2:3. The word "false" comes from the Greek word *plastos*, from which derives the word *plastic*.[4] By replacing the truth with a cheap—but convincing—imitation, false teachers want to make it easy for us to choose heresy instead of orthodoxy, which means "correct opinion."

Second, counterfeit communicators openly deny the truth (2 Peter 2:1). False teachers are often known for what they deny rather than for what they embrace, and they often make their denials sound intelligent and reasonable. They deny the inspiration of Scripture, the sinfulness of humanity, the deity and humanity of Christ, His atoning death and victorious resurrection, salvation by grace through faith alone, and other essential truths of Christianity. Turn on the television, walk into a bookstore, or surf the Internet, and you will see all of these truths being openly denied.

Third, counterfeit communicators unashamedly model immorality (2 Peter 2:2). Here we begin to see some of the motivation behind their denials of the truth. In order to pursue their own fleshly desires, they deny or redefine God's standard of righteousness. From a subtle ridicule of orthodox Christianity to a blatant attack on the resurrection of Christ, these immoral, false teachers label biblical views as outdated, intolerant, and bigoted.

Fourth, counterfeit communicators selfishly represent greed (2 Peter 2:3). They often covetously desire money or have an insatiable ambition for fame. You might recognize novelists or filmmakers motivated by an ungodly agenda who distort history and attack Christianity for fame and fortune. You may see the university professor who exchanges the truths of Christianity for a prestigious chair at an Ivy League school and frequent appearances on television. They are everywhere.

DIGGING DEEPER

Are Counterfeit Communicators Saved?

Are those who willfully and knowingly deny essential truths of the Christian faith saved? According to Peter, the answer is no! They deny "the Master who bought them" and face a "swift destruction" (2 Peter 2:1). Such people are "slaves of corruption" (2 Peter 2:19).

Because Jesus is fully God and fully man, His death on the cross is *potent enough* to pay for the sins of the whole world—including those of false teachers (1 John 2:2), but when it comes to the *application* of that atonement, the benefit of our Lord's death is limited to those who believe (John 3:16–18).

True believers, those who have been saved by faith in Jesus Christ, can doubt, be deceived, and sin. However, they cannot ever utterly fall away from the faith. God, in His powerful grace, keeps them forever in His hand (John 10:29; Romans 8:38–39; Jude 24). Those who *do* appear to "fall away" from the faith, denying the essential truths of Christianity, were never truly saved, as the apostle John says regarding some counterfeit communicators in his own day: "They went out from us, but they were not really of us; for if they had been of us, they would have remained with us; but they went out, so that it would be shown that they all are not of us" (1 John 2:19).

Now that we are aware of the many counterfeit communicators in our midst and we see some of the ways they operate, how can we discern whether what we see on television or in movies; what we read in books, newspapers, or magazines; what we hear on the radio; or even what we are told in church is the truth? How can we avoid being hoodwinked by one of Satan's servants of deceit?

STARTING YOUR JOURNEY

Consider these three practical tips that can help us avoid deception and stay on the way of truth in a world of fiction.

Stop! Refuse to blindly accept someone else's teaching just because it has entertained, persuaded, inspired, or supposedly blessed others. Pause long enough to compare the view being taught with what Scripture teaches. And if the strange teaching challenges the history and authority of the Bible, seek out Christian scholars who will help you become familiar with the other side of the evidence. (Some excellent resources for this can be found in the "Resources for Probing Further" section at the end of this workbook.)

Look! Take a careful look at the life of the main spokesperson of a particular teaching or perspective. Does his or her lifestyle suggest a motivation of greed, fame, power, or the justification of immorality? Never be swayed because someone sounds intelligent or wooed by someone's charisma. Examine not only *what* he or she says, but *why* he or she says it.

Listen! Pay attention to the terms a person uses and how they are defined. Also listen for what's *not* being said. Do not judge truth by how something makes you feel. Often the real truth will make people feel uncomfortable, convicted, or obligated. Lies are often crafted to provide false security, freedom, and excitement. Think critically, and make your judgments according to Scripture.

We all need to be more aware of the false teaching that is so prevalent in our world. We need to be able to identify its errors, motivations, and the potential harm it may cause. Begin to sharpen your discernment by keeping your eyes open over the next week for various forms of media (books, magazines, movies, and so forth) that advocate false or questionable teachings. Once you've identified some of these, ask yourself the following questions.

How do the people behind these forms of media deceitfully present heresy, blatantly deny truth, model immorality, or represent greed? Be specific.

____

____

____

____

____

What about these deceptions is particularly persuasive or attractive?

____

____

____

____

____

Leader Help

Group members should be prepared to bring examples of books, movies, magazine articles, or other forms of media that demonstrate the work of counterfeit communicators. If your group didn't work ahead, feel free to discuss your answers at the beginning of your next meeting.

What is the potential for damage from these forms of deception? Is it serious or mild? Limited or widespread? In what ways?

In this lesson we learned that heresy plagues us today as much or even more than it did in the early church, often appealing to the unwary. We should be motivated to strengthen our own knowledge of the truth, to engage in spiritual battle against heresy, and to look out for the safety of those who may not be aware of the dangers. In the following lessons, we'll take steps toward each of these worthy goals.

Lesson Two

The Acts of the Apostates

Jude 1–4

THE HEART OF THE MATTER

The first time it was read, the tiny, remarkably relevant book of Jude probably fell like the blow of a hammer on the hearts of its audience—condemning the acts of those who opposed the faith and warning the faithful believers. This little, single-chapter letter may be the most dramatic exposé and denunciation of heresy in the entire Bible. It calls us to prepare for battle—to equip our hearts and minds with a deep knowledge of and commitment to the truth.

YOU ARE HERE

The following script is a hypothetical dialogue between a modern-day critic of orthodox Christianity and an unsuspecting Christian. As you read through it, carefully note the historical and theological issues and questions that stand out to you. Circle any statements that challenge your thinking. Consider each statement carefully.

Leader Help

By the end of this lesson, group members should recognize their need to be equipped to stand against false teaching by developing discernment between truth and error, and they should be motivated to begin strengthening their knowledge through personal study.

Leader Help
Rather than simply reading this dialogue as a group, you may choose to have two people read this scripted conversation while others take notes. Then answer the questions together.

"Did you know that Jesus never claimed to be God? In fact, the earliest Christians believed he was just a man—a great rabbi—whose teachings transformed their lives. The church didn't start referring to him as God until generations later."

"Really? I thought He claimed to be God *and* man. He proved Himself to be both when He rose from the dead."

"That's not true. He didn't *literally* rise from the dead. See, the earliest New Testament books were written at least thirty years after Jesus died, and the writers created the myth of the resurrection and other miraculous stories to illustrate deeper spiritual lessons. They're not meant to be taken at face value."

"So Easter never really happened? What about the empty tomb? The eyewitness accounts?"

"Well, *something* happened. But Jesus's body was probably tossed in a mass grave like most of those who were crucified. You see, the myth of the physical resurrection was a way of communicating the reality of our own spiritual awakening. Through his life and death, Jesus inspired his followers to live new lives. Later followers of Jesus described this spiritual and emotional experience in story form—and *voila*, we have the Easter story."

"You mean they lied to us?"

"No, no, no. *Lied* is such a harsh term. The people of the ancient world were accustomed to hearing spiritual truth in the form of mythical stories—remember Greek mythology? The early Christians simply illustrated the meaning of Christianity with stories."

"I don't understand. Did Jesus do what the Gospel writers said He did or not?"

"Listen, it doesn't matter if the events happened or not. What *really* matters is how the stories transform you as you encounter the god- or goddess-consciousness within you and rise to higher levels of spiritual awareness yourself. Did you ever read or see *The Da Vinci Code?*"

"Yeah, but I thought it was fiction."

"Well, the story itself is fiction, but much of the history woven throughout it is true. It's been confirmed by historians and scholars."

"What do you mean?"

"I'm glad you asked. Scholars have shown that the earliest believers didn't really believe Jesus was God—that doctrine was added by later Christians and church leaders. Many viewed his resurrection in spiritual, symbolic terms, rather than understanding it as a literal, physical reality. You see, the earliest followers of Jesus were quite diverse in their beliefs—they didn't believe that just one orthodox view was right and everything else was wrong. The whole idea of orthodoxy and heresy was invented later by the Catholic Church to defeat other forms of Christianity. In fact, we have all sorts of writings and gospels by other Christians that took a more spiritual view of Jesus and the faith."

I want to forewarn you not to get snagged on the hooks of worthless opinions but instead to be fully convinced about the birth and the suffering and the resurrection, which took place during the time of the governorship of Pontius Pilate. These things were truly and most assuredly done by Jesus Christ, our hope, from which may none of you ever be turned aside.[1]

—Ignatius of Antioch (c. AD 110)

"Well then, what happened to all the other Christians and Scriptures?"

"The Catholic Church tried to suppress and destroy them. Their ultimate concerns were power and money. Only in the last hundred years have historians been able to uncover the conspiracy and discover the truth."

"Conspiracy? That sounds like fiction to me. You have to admit it's a little far fetched."

"You've only been exposed to the Catholic Church's version of history. Open your eyes, friend. The truth can't be denied—the traditional form of Christianity is coming to an end."

Consider the historical and theological issues that you marked throughout the dialogue. Which of these arguments have you heard personally in books, movies, television, magazines, or personal conversations? Which are completely new to you?

Leader Help

Your group may struggle with this activity. It is designed to measure just how unprepared we are to fend off theological questions or doctrinal attacks. Encourage your group—many of these topics will be addressed throughout this course of study. For an initial primer on the central doctrines of the Christian faith, see "Digging Deeper" on page 28.

What do you think the average unbeliever today would find appealing about this critic's views? Why?

____

____

____

____

____

Do you feel equipped to address these issues from a Christian perspective? Why or why not?

____

____

____

____

____

DISCOVERING THE WAY

Jesus warned that the end times would be marked by wholesale rejection of the truth (Matthew 24:10–11), and Paul echoed Jesus's resounding alarm (2 Thessalonians 2:3; 1 Timothy 4:1; 2 Timothy 4:3–4). Today we see blatant rejection of the truth throughout our world—how can we stand strong against those who would undermine our faith? How can we keep our feet on the way of dependable truth in a world of deceptive fiction? The book of Jude speaks directly to these questions.

I believe in one God the Father Almighty, Maker of heaven and earth, and of all things visible and invisible.[2]

—The Nicene Creed

The Author's Admonition

Jude was the brother of James and the half-brother of Jesus. Although at one time Jude thought his oldest brother had lost His mind (Mark 3:21), he later described himself as Christ's "bond-servant" (Jude 1). His singular goal in life was to be forever at Jesus's disposal—especially at this critical moment when the faith was coming under attack from all sides.

GETTING TO THE ROOT

The word for *contend* in Jude 3 is *epagonizomai*. It means "to struggle for, to contend for, to exercise great effort and exertion for something. The word was used [to describe] athletic contests and the struggle and effort of the athletes in their games."[3] If you look at this Greek word carefully, you'll see the root from which we get our English word *agonize*. The word picture brings to mind two wrestlers *contending* for the prize of victory.

Read Jude 1. How does Jude's unique relationship to Jesus and James give him special authority to write this letter to believers?

____

____

____

____

____

According to Jude 3, what had he intended to write about?

____

What topic did Jude choose to write about instead?

____

____

____

What does this indicate about the circumstances surrounding Jude? In other words, why did he write this letter?

____

____

____

____

____

What did Jude mean when he wrote about "the faith?" First, "the faith" doesn't refer to the personal faith of individual believers but to the Christian faith taught by the apostles and contained in Scripture—the central doctrines of the faith that were later summarized in the early creeds and confessions (see "Digging Deeper" on page 28). Second, this faith was "once for all" delivered from God through Jesus Christ. Though it may be better understood and explained throughout history, the faith cannot be added to, taken from, or molded to suit each generation's lifestyles. Finally, the faith was delivered "to the saints"—to every believer but *only* to believers. It was not given for the world, the critics, or the novelists to twist and reinterpret. The faith was intended for every believer to understand, study, and live—not only the theologian and pastor but also the little child who just trusted Christ with simple faith.

How can believers with personal faith in Christ grow in "the faith"—that is, in the central doctrines taught by Christ and His apostles? Be specific.

What are some benefits of growing stronger in the faith?

Read the following Scripture passages and note what they teach about the faith.

1 Corinthians 16:13

Philippians 1:27–28

Colossians 1:21–23

1 Timothy 6:20–21

Do you see any particular commands to follow or instructions to obey in these Scriptures? List several action words that summarize what believers should do in response to these passages.

The Apostates

Apostates are people who willfully and deliberately defect from the faith. Although they once appeared to agree with the church on the doctrines of Christianity, they never really trusted Christ for their eternal salvation. With arrogance and defiance in their hearts, they purposefully oppose the central teachings of the Christian faith and plant seeds of doubt, division, and dissension among believers.

Read Jude 4. How did Jude describe the apostates?

Deliberately seeking to live with integrity, the true apostles always kept a high profile, teaching and practicing their doctrine publicly (2 Timothy 2:2). In contrast, the early apostates mischievously spread sinister words and works behind the scenes, poisoning the core of Christian truth in at least two ways. First, they used "grace" as a license for loose living, converting it from freedom to obey Christ to freedom to sin (Romans 6:15–23). Second, fueled by their perversions, they denied the person and work of Jesus Christ.

STARTING YOUR JOURNEY

It's rare to turn on the television or watch a movie without seeing at least one Christian truth crucified on the screen. In the media, on the college campus, in the workplace, in the newspapers and magazines, and even in churches that have rejected the authority of the Scriptures, the faith is under constant attack. The world scoffs at the essential doctrines of the faith, lampooning Christians and ridiculing Scripture. The result? Inch by inch, the doctrinal foundation of many unsuspecting believers has been eaten away.

How about you? Would you be able to instantly identify false teaching if you read it in a novel or saw it in a movie? Would you be able to answer a scoffer if he maligned your faith? Would you be able to critique the criticisms of the Ivy League scholars who strike at the historical roots of the Christian faith?

I believe . . . in one Lord Jesus Christ, the only-begotten Son of God, begotten of His Father before all worlds, God of God, Light of Light, very God of very God, begotten, not made, being of one substance with the Father, by whom all things were made; Who for us men and for our salvation came down from heaven, and was incarnate by the Holy Spirit of the Virgin Mary.[4]

—The Nicene Creed

I believe in the Holy Spirit, the holy Christian church, the communion of saints, the forgiveness of sins, the resurrection of the body, and the life everlasting.[5]

—The Apostles Creed

DIGGING DEEPER
The Center of Theology

Christianity is certainly diverse. In fact, some of the differences between various denominations have been the subject of much disagreement, debate, and even conflict through the centuries. However, all true Christian churches, denominations, and teachers are now and have always been in agreement over the central doctrines of the faith.

Christians from the earliest days of the church to the present day have held to these core biblical doctrines of the faith: the infallibility of Scripture as the final authority in faith and practice; one eternal, triune God in three persons: Father, Son, and Holy Spirit; the absolute deity and perfect humanity of Jesus Christ, His virgin birth, sinless life, substitutionary death, bodily resurrection, and literal, future return; the special creation and fall of humanity; salvation by grace through faith; and the eternal life of believers and condemnation of unbelievers. Those who have strayed far from this center of orthodoxy have been regarded as outside of the true Christian faith.

Some liberal theologians and critical scholars want to advocate further diversity in Christianity by including teachings that deny the essential truths of historic Christianity—the faith once for all entrusted to the saints (Jude 3). These teachers, bent on pluralism and relativism, deliberately emphasize a so-called "radical diversity" in the early centuries of Christianity and the dozens of false views about Christ. They want us to embrace as brothers and sisters the varieties of "Christianity" that have no part in the central truths of the faith. However, true Christians today must stand with the faithful saints of old who fought against heresy rather than tolerated or embraced it.

It's clear that Jude regarded the Christian faith as a single body of truth worth defending. Avoiding the battle is not an option for believers today, for our culture increasingly brings the battle to our own doorsteps. The conversation at the beginning of this lesson may be fictional, but the views expressed about Jesus and the Bible are very real.

What can you do when you hear these attacks from both entertainers and educators? Prepare to identify the counterfeit by learning the truth well. Equipping yourself for this task requires a two-pronged approach. The first step is to study the Bible, its doctrines, and its personal application on a regular basis. Second, study books and articles that defend the faith against the criticisms of historians, scholars, and, yes, even novelists. You cannot prepare adequately for the battle if you are not aware of the issues you will encounter.

Leader Help

Each member of the group should select a resource from this list and bring at least one insight gleaned from the reading to the next group meeting. Be sure to remind the group that they don't have to read an entire book to do this assignment.

Begin to strengthen your roots in the faith so you'll be able to discern the way of truth in a world of fiction. Consult the list of resources in "Resources for Probing Further" on pages 239–244 and select a work from one of the first five numbered sections, including works on *The Da Vinci Code*, Christian theology and doctrine, defenses of the faith, church history, and the early Christian writings.

After reading or reviewing your selection over the next week or so, return to the hypothetical dialogue at the beginning of this lesson. Based on your study, what issues might you begin to address or answer?

Do you have a clear "sense of the center" in Christian theology? What would you personally say are the central, most important truths of the Christian faith that all true believers must hold?

How does your list differ from the doctrines described in "Digging Deeper" on page 28? Pay close attention to these differences. They will provide excellent guidelines for your future study.

In this lesson we have discovered the need to be equipped to stand against false teaching by developing discernment between doctrinal truth and error. Are you ready to strengthen your knowledge through personal study? It won't always be easy, but in a time when error is flaunted as fact, we must diligently follow the way of truth in a world of fiction.

Lesson Three

Why Bother to Battle?

Jude 5–16

THE HEART OF THE MATTER

Though Jude had intended to present a calm, calculated explanation of the Christian life, the Spirit of God moved him to unleash a blistering exposé of heresy and to exhort his readers to contend earnestly for the faith. His tiny letter provides helpful guidelines for standing firm against the tempting trends of our times. Unlike many today who tolerate heresy to keep the peace, Jude demonstrated clearly that the battle is worth the bother.

YOU ARE HERE

Taking a stand for the truth is not always easy, especially for those who might be natural peacemakers, who fear the consequences of disagreement, or who want to avoid confrontation. Nevertheless, circumstances often call us to battle for the essentials of the faith even if we feel uncomfortable.

Leader Help

By the end of this lesson, group members should understand the importance of challenging false teaching both inside and outside the church, personally accepting the call to engage false teachers with an attitude of love.

Leader Help

In a setting with limited time, a group could not possibly discuss each of the situations presented in this group discussion. Try to select one or two that fit the dynamics of your group best, or if your group worked ahead, discuss the questions that follow these hypothetical situations.

In the following situations, what would be your typical natural response?

1. A guest preacher or teacher at your church suggests that the apostle Paul probably didn't write all of the letters bearing his name; instead, he or she proposes that these epistles were probably written years after his death by one of his followers.
2. An unbelieving friend asks you to read a novel that attacks Christianity because he or she knows you are a believer and wants to discuss the book with you.
3. A man and woman knock at your door offering literature that presents the Trinity as a non-biblical doctrine. They ask if you would be interested in scheduling a Bible study with them to discuss the matter.
4. A Christian university you have supported for years hires a teacher who is known for his controversial views. He suggests that doctrines such as the virgin birth, deity, and resurrection of Christ are meant to be understood spiritually rather than literally.

In general, would you tend to engage these errors, or would you tend to avoid confrontation?

Explain why you typically respond this way.

Would you feel more comfortable confronting error in some of these scenarios and not others? If so, which ones? Why?

DISCOVERING THE WAY

The daily regimen on a military base is as well-trimmed as a new recruit's haircut. The routine consists of endless drills and training for battles that everyone hopes will never happen. Yet, if an enemy threatens the nation, the well-trained soldiers snap into action, ready to fight and even die so future generations may live in peace.

In this way, the military serves as an excellent example for the church. We pray that enemies will never infiltrate our ranks with destructive doctrines or attack the faith of our weaker brothers and sisters with lies. If they do, however, we must be ready to fight for our beliefs—not with physical weapons but with spiritual weapons of knowledge, wisdom, faith, hope, and love.

In his brief epistle, Jude rallied the troops with this cry: "Contend earnestly for the faith" (Jude 3). Like a good field commander, Jude realized the importance of stirring up our fighting spirit, motivating believers to be involved in the battle.

A Brief Review

The particular invaders who rallied Jude's ire were twisting grace into a license to sin as well as denying the person and work of Christ. This description matches a particular category of heresies that eventually became known as Gnosticism (see "Doorway to History" on page 8). The various groups of Gnostics blended Christianity with Greek philosophy, Middle Eastern religions, and even Jewish mysticism. Fundamentally, they taught that our physical body is evil, and our spirit is good. According to theologian Millard Erickson, this teaching led to two extremes:

> Whereas some Gnostics drew the conclusion that, the body being evil, a strict asceticism should be practiced, others concluded that what is done with the body is spiritually irrelevant, and hence engaged in licentious behavior.[1]

Apparently, teachers like the latter type of Gnostics had infiltrated the church, claiming that their righteousness in Christ freed them to do as they pleased. One commentator notes, "Those who fussed about sexual purity seemed to them astonishingly naïve."[2] They also taught strange doctrines about Christ, denying His humanity and assuming that He had merely a ghost-like existence.

Having established a strong following within the church, Gnostics struck at the heart of the Christian faith. Like Paul Revere sounding the alarm, Jude roused the troops: "The enemy is upon us! Now is the time for action!"

Read Jude 4 and 5. In contrast with Gnostics—who taught that a "special" knowledge was necessary for the spiritually elite—what did Jude say about the knowledge believers have as members of the Christian faith?

What do each of the following passages teach about the wisdom and knowledge believers have in Christ?

1 Corinthians 2:10–16

Leader Help

This series of questions can be summarized or answered as a group depending upon time constraints. Or you may break into two or four smaller groups and divide up the passages. Each small group may then present their answers to the group as a whole.

Ephesians 1:8–9, 17

James 1:5; 3:17

1 John 2:20, 27

Reasons to Fight

Believers in the true Christ who study the true Scriptures and fellowship in a true church already have the infallible sources of true knowledge and wisdom. Knowing this, Jude provided four essential reasons to join in the fight for the true faith.

First, we know that heretics face certain doom.

Read Jude 5–7. Jude listed three Old Testament examples to shed light on the destiny of the apostates. What were they?

Based on these examples, do you think Jude regarded these heretics as truly saved or as imposters? Why?

The implication of Jude's strong warning is clear: Refuse to sympathize with those whom God condemns. Why hear them out or entertain the idea of following them when their path has led *them* to death and will just as surely lead others there as well? It is absurd to think we could find the way of life in those who are spiritually dead or follow them to find the way of truth in a world of pure fiction. If

There are two ways, one of life and one of death, and there is a great difference between these two ways.[3]

—The Didache (c. AD 100)

apostates attack what we believe, we must be prepared to fight for the purity of God's message. It's a matter of eternal life or death.

Second, false teachers blaspheme.

Read Jude 8–10. Of what specific actions did Jude accuse these false teachers?

The characteristics of ancient heretics are similar to modern humanists and skeptics—from whom much anti-Christian criticism comes. They presuppose the utter independence and sovereignty of humans. They reject the lordship and reality of God. They embrace naturalism and reject the supernatural. As a result, not only do they denigrate the resurrection of Christ and His deity but their presuppositions prevent them from regarding such things as *possible*. These unbelievers have made up their minds before examining the evidence.

Third, the religion of the apostates is empty.

Read Jude 11–13. As you consider the montage of metaphors in verses 12–13, how would you describe the character of these heretics and the nature of their teachings? How do Jude's images make you feel about the heretics?

____

____

____

____

____

The errors of the apostates were manifold. Cain endorsed a religion that offered God the fruit of human works rather than a blood sacrifice (Genesis 4:1–7; Hebrews 9:22; 11:4). Balaam set out to peddle his prophecies for money (Numbers 22; Deuteronomy 23:3–4; Nehemiah 13:2; 2 Peter 2:15–16). Korah was a Levite who led a mutiny against the authority of Moses and Aaron (Numbers 16:1–33). Similarly, the apostates of Jude's day were denying the reality of Christ's atonement, seeking financial gain, and rebelling against spiritual authority in the church. Things haven't changed much, have they?

Finally, heretics live godless lives and seek to spread their evil ways among others.

Read Jude 14–16. How many times is "ungodly" used to describe these heretics?

What types of ungodly attitudes and actions do you see in verse 16 that would cause Jude to speak such harsh condemnation in verse 15?

A Balanced Response

Jude's purpose was to instill in his audience a deep sense of righteous anger against apostates. Has it worked? Are you ready to take on these apostates? Before you do, beware. If you are not careful, righteous indignation could boil over and become uncontrolled hostility. Too quickly, calm confrontations can explode into name-calling and shouting matches. And then nobody wins.

How can you fight passionately for the faith without losing your head? The key is to be thoroughly prepared. The most persuasive argument in any debate is the truth; so use it. Know where you stand doctrinally. Know where false teachers stand, too. And don't be afraid to take a stand. You may be the one flickering flame in the darkness, the only voice in a crowd of dissenters . . . but you will never be alone. God's Spirit and His Word are always with you, no matter where you go.

DOORWAY TO HISTORY
Early Contenders

Those who earnestly contend for the faith today stand in a long line of saints who have fought for the central truths of Christianity against false teachers and bloodthirsty tyrants from the beginning. While most modern Christians know of the martyrdoms of the apostles, many are unaware of those who came later—those who battled heresy, confronted paganism, and challenged the policies of persecution, often under the threat of brutal execution. Let's examine a few of these courageous believers who lost their lives because they dared to take a stand and whose writings survived as testimonies of their faithfulness.

Ignatius of Antioch (martyred c. AD 110). While on his way to martyrdom in Rome, Ignatius wrote seven letters to various churches, including Ephesus, Smyrna, and Rome. He challenged the false teachings of Judaizers and docetists, who denied the true incarnation of Christ. He called for unity within the church in regard to the true doctrine of Christ and the essentials of the gospel.

Continued on next page

But when the magistrate persisted and said, "Swear the oath, and I will release you; revile Christ," Polycarp replied, "For eighty-six years I have been his servant, and he has done me no wrong. How can I blaspheme my King who saved me?"

But as he continued to insist, saying, "Swear by the Genius of Caesar," he answered: "If you vainly suppose that I will swear by the Genius of Caesar, as you request, and pretend not to know who I am, listen carefully: I am a Christian."[4]

—The Martyrdom of Polycarp (c. AD 155)

Continued from previous page

Polycarp of Smyrna (martyred c. AD. 155). A friend of Ignatius and student of the apostle John, Polycarp was a long-time pastor of Smyrna. He battled heretics like Marcion and advanced the gospel of Christ, eventually suffering martyrdom in his eighties.

Justin the Martyr (martyred c. AD 165). Justin was a convert to Christianity from Greek philosophy. He wrote several defenses of Christianity against both pagans and Jews, and he combated Gnostics and Marcionites. As his name indicates, Justin was ultimately martyred for his faith at the hands of the Romans.

Irenaeus of Lyons (martyred c. AD 200). Originally from Asia Minor, Irenaeus was a disciple of Polycarp who lived in Rome before serving as a pastor in Lyons (modern-day France). There he wrote the massive, five-book *Against All Heresies*, in which he demonstrated the true Christian faith and identified the errors of the heretical groups of his day, especially the Gnostics.

STARTING YOUR JOURNEY

Engaging false teachers is not an easy task. A believer must be prepared not only mentally with the right answers but spiritually with the right attitude. Some who are prepared mentally have the wrong heart. Some who are prepared spiritually have the wrong answers. Mental preparation requires knowledge. Spiritual preparation requires wisdom. And both are absolutely essential.

Are you currently involved in any situations in which you could engage false teaching? Where? You may want to review the hypothetical situations in "You Are Here" on pages 33–34 for various circumstances believers might encounter.

Leader Help
Although these questions apply primarily to individuals, group members should discuss their particular situations and encourage each other with wisdom and insight.

Consider what you have learned in this lesson so far. What should you do in your specific situation?

Do you feel equipped to take a stand in this matter? If not, what do you lack: knowledge or wisdom? Why do you feel this way?

If you lack knowledge, how can you continue to increase your knowledge of the truth? You may want to return to the suggestions in the "Resources for Probing Further" section at the end of this workbook.

Read Proverbs 2:1–9. If you lack wisdom, what should you do?

The following passages from Proverbs provide precious wisdom for those who want to engage false teachings. Read them all, then choose two or three to memorize.

Proverbs 15:1
Proverbs 15:28
Proverbs 18:13
Proverbs 25:15

Note how the following passages urge believers to engage unbelievers with both knowledge and wisdom. How could these passages apply to the specific situations in which you should stand against false teaching?

Ephesians 4:14–15

Colossians 4:5–6

1 Peter 3:14–16

In this lesson we've seen the importance of challenging false teachings both inside and outside the church. Hopefully, you've been personally challenged to engage false teachers and correct their teachings in love. Though you may not have encountered false teachers lately, it's only a matter of time before they cross your path. Will you be ready to take them on? Will you be willing?

Lesson Four

Get Your Act Together!

Jude 17–25

THE HEART OF THE MATTER

A battle against heresy has been raging for centuries with drum-like monotony and increasing intensity. The church was still in its infancy when the battle began. Having exposed the false prophets and twisted teachers of his own day, Jude exhorted his readers to stay on target themselves, to get their act together, to stand firm in the faith against all opposition—and to come to the aid of the weary soldiers who have been led astray by false teaching. His message is the same for us as we stand for unchanging truth in a world of fiction.

Leader Help

By the end of this lesson, group members should acknowledge their responsibility to fellow believers who have been deceived by heresy and be motivated to identify and help others who have been led astray.

YOU ARE HERE

Picture this. While you're at church, a dear lady approaches you with a heartfelt prayer request: "Could you pray for my son John? He's decided not to attend church anymore. He read some books recently about where the Bible came from and the early years of the church, and now he's having doubts about Christianity. He asks questions I can't answer. I've always had a simple faith. I don't even know what he's talking about. How can I help him? I'm so afraid that he's lost his faith, and I don't know what to do."

How would you respond to this woman? Be specific.

Do you think faithful believers have an obligation to help other believers who doubt? Why?

Do you tend to avoid interaction with those who doubt, or do you seek to embrace and encourage them? Explain your answer.

DISCOVERING THE WAY

In 1940, as the war against Hitler raged in Europe, British ships and boats rescued more than 300,000 Allied troops who had been surrounded by the Germans at Dunkirk, France. Thirty thousand French and British soldiers were killed or taken prisoner, but Winston Churchill, the prime minister of Great Britain, stood his ground. In a speech to the House of Commons on June 4, 1940, he said these famous words:

> We shall not flag or fail. We shall go on to the end. We shall fight in France, we shall fight on the seas and oceans, we shall fight with growing confidence and growing strength in the air, we shall defend our island, whatever the cost may be, we shall fight on the beaches, we shall fight on the landing grounds, we shall fight in the fields and in the streets, we shall fight in the hills; we shall never surrender.[1]

> Therefore let us leave behind the worthless speculation of the crowd and their false teachings, and let us return to the word delivered to us from the beginning.[2]
>
> —Polycarp of Smyrna (c. AD 110)

With similar resolve and determination, Jude exhorted Christians to "contend earnestly for the faith" (Jude 3). Today, heresy storms our own shores. The preservation of truth and morality hangs in the balance. At the end of Jude's letter, he made a final appeal to the soldiers of the faith in the midst of a raging battle against the onslaught of false teachers.

A Serious Situation

Jude worried that his readers might become spiritual casualties—for good reason. They were already enduring physical oppression from the Romans, who, at the time, were stepping up their persecution. Now they had to weather the insidious assaults of the apostates (2 Timothy 3:6–9; 4:3–4). Jude fervently pleaded with his audience, exhorting them to fight for their beliefs.

Although the circumstances have changed since the first century, the broader issue remains very serious. Many enemies of Christ lurk outside and inside the church, waiting to assail our faith. That's why, once we've girded ourselves with a protective fortress of truth, we must take action on behalf of other believers around us.

Jude's Final Instructions for the Troops

As Jude drew his short letter to a close, he issued at least four commands to the troops in Christ's army: remember your training (Jude 17–19), keep in shape (20–21), have mercy on the war-torn (22), and save the defectors (23).

Read 2 Peter 3:3–7 and Jude 17–19. Notice that Jude deliberately echoes Peter's warning. Why do you think Jude wanted to remind his readers that these events would indeed take place?

What opportunity did Peter give believers by warning them in advance that false prophets and teachers would come?

What were Jude's readers supposed to remember?

DIGGING DEEPER

Orthodoxy and Heresy

In the twentieth century the distinction between "orthodoxy" and "heresy" began to come under attack. Unbelieving historians claim that these are prejudicial terms which represent an orthodox bias against diverse Christian groups. They assert that in our modern age of pluralism, tolerance, and diversity, we should do away with such mean-spirited labels. After all, they say, if there's no such thing as "orthodoxy," we should stop calling others "heretics." Maybe you've seen some of these scholars interviewed for television specials, or perhaps you've read their claims in news magazines.[3]

Along with this new emphasis, some scholars have suggested that not only was early Christianity characterized by radical diversity and conflict between Christians, but what became orthodoxy was only one view of a multitude of groups claiming to be the true followers of Christ. These modern-day skeptics teach that one group eventually suppressed all opposition and selected only the New Testament books that agreed with this dominant group's theology. In the process, the skeptics claim, the "orthodox" church stomped out the rich diversity of early Christianity and declared the church's opponents to be "heretics." And who are the modern heirs of these orthodox bullies who rewrote history to support their power? Those who believe the Bible as the inspired Word of God and hold to the classic doctrine of the Christian faith!

It's important to recognize that these scholars who talk about "diversity," "intolerance," "suppression," and even "rewriting history" presuppose that the resurrection of Christ is false; therefore, they can't believe that one true form of Christian teaching exists. They are also often driven by modern-day agendas that emphasize religious pluralism, tolerance, and even immoral lifestyles. Their claims—though dressed in the garb of intellectualism and Ivy League respectability—are based not on the clear facts of history but upon biased presuppositions common in our day.[4]

In the Bible, the apostles warned against false teachers, whose presence would be a certainty in the last days (Acts 20:28–30; 1 Timothy 4:1–2; 2 Peter 3:3–4). By expecting them, we're less likely to become paralyzed and disillusioned when they invade our church. We take away the advantage of surprise, and if we can spot them through their camouflage, the battle is partly won.

Wherefore they must be opposed at all points, if perchance, by cutting off their retreat, we may succeed in turning them back to the truth. For, though it is not an easy thing for a soul under the influence of error to repent, yet, on the other hand, it is not altogether impossible to escape from error when the truth is brought alongside it.[5]

—Irenaeus of Lyons
(c. AD 185)

Jude provided five specific characteristics to identify false prophets (Jude 18–19). Which of the following have you seen or experienced either inside or outside the Christian church?

___ Mocking people who ridicule the Christian faith and Scriptures

___ Immoral people who undercut truth to justify their actions

___ Divisive people who sow seeds of discord and criticism in the church

___ Worldly-minded people who reinterpret the Christian faith in accordance with the world's values

___ Spiritually-bankrupt people who, though they appear genuine for a time, prove to be false

Read Jude 20–21. This passage contains one imperative (command) and three participles that tell us how we should be fulfilling the imperative. Place the corresponding words in the list below:

Keep yourselves in the love of God . . .

1. ________________ yourselves up on your most holy faith.

2. ________________ in the Holy Spirit.

3. ________________ for the mercy of our Lord Jesus Christ to eternal life.

How do these three actions help us to be strong in the love of God?

How will being strong in the love of God help us as we seek to preserve our own faith against false teachers as well as come to the aid of others?

Read Jude 22–23. Carefully identify the condition of each type of person mentioned, then list the corresponding responses specified by these verses.

Condition	Response
1. ______________	______________
______________	______________
2. ______________	______________
______________	______________
3. ______________	______________
______________	______________

Leader Help
This question gives group members an opportunity to encourage intervention through personal testimonies. They can be a powerful means of motivating others to action.

Have you ever helped a believer in one of these conditions? If so, describe your response and the end result.

____

____

____

____

____

Looking back on that experience, would you have handled any part of it differently? Why? What would you change?

Final Benediction for the Troops

Jude's closing benediction communicated God's protection during present and future battles. With stirring rhetoric, he called out to the troops who were engaged in spiritual warfare.

Read Jude 24–25 out loud. Why do you think Jude chose to end his letter against false teachers this way?

STARTING YOUR JOURNEY

In previous lessons we studied the reality of false teaching, discovered several ways to equip ourselves for this battle, and learned how to engage those who propagate fantasies as fact. Now we'll focus on coming to the aid of the fellow soldier wounded in combat, paralyzed by fear and doubt, or dazed by the trauma of the conflict. How can you minister to those who have been disillusioned because of seeds of doubt or weakened because of the claims of false teachers? Several practical steps will aid us as we seek to rescue a wayward brother or sister caught in the snare of false teaching.

First, listen to the person. Don't shun or avoid him or her. Find out exactly what's causing the doubts. He or she may have experienced more than just a seed of untruth planted by a deceptive source. In fact, sometimes these seeds are only able to take root because deeper problems have prepared the soil. Has the person been through a faith-challenging struggle with suffering or loss? Is he blinded by the temptation of a particular sin? Is she under the relentless ridicule of people she loves or respects? Has he or she been wounded in the context of the church, perhaps through observing the moral fall of a spiritual authority or experiencing a lack of acceptance or care in the midst of a spiritual, emotional, or physical crisis? Be sensitive and watch for deeper issues.

Second, keep in contact with your friend and meet with him or her regularly. A very wise person once said, "They won't care how much you know until they know how much you care." You are intervening out of love and care for the person's spiritual well-being. Don't browbeat or condescend. Take time to build your relationship on a foundation of honesty and accountability. You are far more likely to make a difference in that person's life if you treat him or her with love and respect, taking the time to understand his or her deep struggle with these issues, and sharing the weight of his or her burden.

Consider each of the following passages. How should believers help those who are wandering from the fold?

Galatians 6:1–2

____

____

1 Thessalonians 5:14

____

____

Hebrews 12:12–13

____

____

James 5:19–20

____

____

Third, approach the problem with outside help from experts. If it's an emotional or moral problem, locate resources that address these issues. Sometimes merely demonstrating your concern about the person at this level will go a long way toward helping him or her.

If the problem is intellectual, find resources that address the specific need. Get two copies—one for the person you're trying to help and another for you—then, if the person is willing, agree to meet together to discuss the issue. Come alongside him or her rather than talking down to the person. Work through the problem together.

Finally, after several meetings, you may notice that the person's heart does not change or even hardens toward the truth. (Be sure to carefully discern between a hard heart and simple discouragement or weakness.) In that case you may have to confront the individual with a strong warning and appeal for repentance (James 5:19–20). You may even want to involve other mutual friends. If your friend remains hardened or rejects your intervention, you must "have mercy with fear" (Jude 23). In other words, *keep showing love and continue to pray, turning him or her over to the Lord's care and discipline*.

Do you know anyone who has been influenced by false teachings or who has entertained doubts about the faith because of exposure to cults, scholarly criticism, or even books or movies that undermine Christian truth? If so, write his or her name or initials here and begin to pray for this individual.

In response to this study, what will you do this week to begin ministering to this person's spiritual needs? Review the suggestions on pages 60–62, then develop a plan of action you can implement immediately.

What outside resources have you used that might be helpful for this person?

Leader Help

Although the answers to this series of questions are quite personal, working through these as a group can be extremely helpful. Encourage group members to share their own experiences and also suggest resources or courses of action that other group members may not have considered.

In what areas might you need to build up your knowledge to better minister to those who are struggling with spiritual or theological issues? Revisit the recommendations in "Resources for Probing Further," starting on page 239.

Each one of us is responsible for the spiritual safety of our Christian brothers and sisters—and therefore we're also accountable to intervene when they're in danger of deception. Have you been motivated to help others who may have been led astray by Satan's sweet-sounding propaganda? Has God placed somebody in your path today? If so, don't delay. Get your act together now!

Lesson Five

One Library of Living Truth

Selected Scriptures

THE HEART OF THE MATTER

Critics and contenders of Scripture have been around for thousands of years. For millennia, believers have seen false "scriptures" come and go, have defended the true library of living truth (the Bible) against countless attacks, and have confounded those who would twist its meaning. Even in the midst of this clamorous conflict, those who listen can hear the clear, harmonious tones of the Bible's distinct symphony. It is a diverse library of books with one common theme: the salvation that comes through the person and work of Jesus Christ.

YOU ARE HERE

The Nag Hammadi Library . . . The Qumran Library . . . The Apocrypha—have you ever heard of these collections of ancient writings? How about the titles of some of their volumes: The Gospel of Thomas . . . The Apocalypse of Adam . . . The Thunder, Perfect Mind . . . Trimorphic Protennoia . . . The War Rule

Leader Help

By the end of this lesson, group members should understand the main theme, general structure, and the origin of the Bible, and they should feel more confident in the reliability of Scripture as an infallible source of truth.

. . . The First Apocalypse of James. Are these "lost scriptures" part of your Bible? If not, do you wonder whether you might be missing something?

You may have heard of the Gnostic Gospels or the Dead Sea Scrolls in movies or documentaries. The ancient world was filled with competing "scriptures" claiming to add new revelations to the Jewish and Christian faiths. Why don't our own Bibles include these writings? Who made the decision to reject them? Did they have good reasons to do so? What makes our own Bible so special? We'll begin answering these questions in this lesson and the next, but let's first focus on the beauty and uniqueness of our own library of living truth.

Unlike the self-contradictory myths and legends of the Nag Hammadi Library of the Gnostic sects, the Christian Bible has stood the test of time. That's not to say the Bible hasn't had its critics. In fact, the battle over the Bible has intensified over the years. Today, scholars attack the Old Testament for advocating slavery, ruthless violence, the death penalty, and animal sacrifice. They ridicule the New Testament for claiming Jesus as the only way to God, for criticizing Jews for rejecting their Messiah, and for condemning non-Christians to hell. In a world that challenges the very concept of objective truth at every turn, a book that Christians claim to be a library of living truth can be the object of intense hatred. Books abound that claim to expose the Bible's myths, catalogue its errors, and challenge its origins. And other libraries both ancient and modern still compete for a place in that exclusive category of sacred Scripture.

What are some criticisms of Scripture (or criticisms of particular teachings or doctrines of Christianity) you've heard lately? Where or from whom have you heard them? Discuss what's at the root of each criticism.

In thirty words or less, how would you answer each of the following three questions:

Where did the Bible come from?

Why do you trust the Bible?

Leader Help

Group members may want to be on the lookout for examples of criticisms of Scripture in books, newspapers, or magazines. They can bring these examples to the next group meeting for discussion.

What's the Bible all about?

How do you think being able to answer these questions helps some people to have confidence in the Bible, in Christ, and in the truth of the Christian faith?

How could the inability to answer these questions lead some people into doubt, confusion, and unbelief?

DISCOVERING THE WAY

In AD 303, the emperor Diocletian issued an edict to destroy the Scriptures and to stop Christians from worshiping the one, true God. Twenty-five years later, Constantine, who succeeded Diocletian, ordered copies of these very same Scriptures to be prepared at the government's expense!

In the 1700s, the French philosopher Voltaire announced his belief that in one hundred years from his time, Christianity would be swept from existence. Ironically, only fifty years after Voltaire's death, the Geneva Bible Society used his printing press to produce stacks of Bibles out of Voltaire's own home!

The voices of Diocletian, Voltaire, and countless other critics of the Bible are now mere whispers in history, while the symphony of Scripture plays on. In a constantly changing world where fiction sometimes overshadows fact, Christians must equip themselves with a knowledge not only of the Bible's content but also of where the Bible came from and why we can trust it. Let's start with some general information about the splendid symphony of Scripture.

A thousand times over, the death knell of the Bible has been sounded, the funeral procession formed, the inscription cut on the tombstone, and the committal read. But somehow the corpse never stays put.[1]

—Bernard Ramm

GETTING TO THE ROOT

The word *Bible* actually finds its roots in the Greek word for the papyrus plant, *biblos*. In the ancient Near East, sheets of papyrus were used as paper. As early as the second century, Christians were using the plural form, *biblia*, when referring to their writings.[2] And the word kept traveling through Latin and on into Old French, until it finally reached English as "Bible."[3]

General Information about the Bible

Though a great symphony is performed with instruments played by various musicians, it's still one piece of music, usually written by a single composer. Similarly, the Bible is a library of many books written by many different human authors, but it can rightly be called one book since it was inspired by one heavenly Author—God—and has one main message.

Leader Help

Though intended for individual study, this survey of Scriptures could be used in group time by splitting your group into pairs or smaller groups and assigning each group two or three passages to read and discuss. Have each subgroup share their findings with the rest of the group.

What do the following passages reveal about the origin of biblical writings?

Exodus 24:4; Deuteronomy 31:9

____

____

Isaiah 30:8

____

____

Jeremiah 36:2, 4, 18

Daniel 7:1

Luke 1:1–4

John 21:24–25

Revelation 1:11, 19; 22:18–19

Having examined the variety of ways in which Scripture was written by different authors, do you think the original readers would have had to be convinced of its truthfulness? Why or why not?

TRUTH OR FICTION?
Did a Council of Bishops Vote on Your Bible?

There are a lot of views about how the ancient writings actually became part of the Bible. Some have said that, for political and theological reasons, a council of bishops voted on these particular books out of hundreds of competing writings. Others say the church ran each book through a rigorous test to determine whether it was inspired. The issue of "canonicity" of the books of the Bible is an important topic. (The word *canon* in this context means a "rule" or "standard.") Sorting out fact from fiction in this matter will help strengthen our confidence that the Bible we hold in our hands contains only the books that are meant to be there—and none that don't belong.

Because Christians received the Old Testament canon from the Jews, there was little debate regarding what should be included. So, for the very earliest Christians, "Scripture" consisted of the Old Testament books as we have them in our Bibles today. However, during the first sixty years of the church (until about AD 100), important documents by Spirit-led apostles and prophets were still being written. The consolidation of these various writings into what we call the New Testament took some time.

How did this occur? The Christian leaders and communities to whom the apostles and prophets originally wrote knew which books were *authentic* (written by a true apostle or prophet), *true* (the information was reliable), and therefore *authoritative* (the apostles had been given authority to lead the church, so their words were commands from God). Almost immediately these apostolic writings began to be copied and passed around to neighboring and distant churches. Very soon, churches began to use these "New Testament" writings in teaching and worship. So for most of the books, there was little question about whether or not they were authoritative for the faith and practice of the churches.[4]

Even when we hear about "disputed" books, we should actually be encouraged rather than discouraged because this indicates that the early church leaders were extremely cautious regarding writings about which they were uncertain. However, once they were able to research the origin and contents of the books, they reached a consensus of what was to be accepted as authoritative. The affirmation of our present New Testament canon at the Council of Carthage (AD 397) was not a vote on these books over competing documents but an acknowledgment of the writings that Christians all over the world had already accepted.[5]

Organization of the Bible

Any great musical composition has structure—deliberate organization that enhances the development and presentation of the whole. And so it is with Scripture. The two main sections are the thirty-nine books of the Old Testament and the twenty-seven books of the New Testament. Jesus Christ in His person and work represents the center of God's revelation. The Old Testament points to Christ by revealing humanity's need for a Savior and foreshadows and foretells His coming. The New Testament presents Him in all His fullness as the Savior of humankind.

Leader Help
To best utilize the following activity in a group setting, write the group's answers on the board for each passage, then summarize the common theme based on the group's observations.

What do the following passages tell us about the theme of the Bible?

Luke 24:27

Romans 1:1–2

1 Corinthians 15:3–4

Leader Help
Depending on your group's specific needs, you may choose whether or not to spend time studying these descriptions of the various genres in the Bible.

The Old and New Testament books can be categorized based on the types of writings. Let's summarize the various types of Old Testament books.

Legal (Genesis through Deuteronomy): These five books reveal the fall and repeated failure of early humanity, as well as God's righteous requirements as revealed through His Law—a Law that demonstrates humankind's need for a Savior.

Historical (Joshua through Esther): These twelve books trace the development, disobedience, downfall, and deliverance of the nation of Israel—highlighting the need for a perfect, incorruptible Prophet, Priest, and King.

Poetical (Job through Song of Solomon): These five books present profound truth and wisdom through poetry and praise, foreshadowing the coming of the praiseworthy personification of truth and wisdom, Jesus Christ.

Prophetical (Isaiah through Malachi): The seventeen prophetic books call on God's people to be faithful to the old covenant of the Law as well as the promise of a future new covenant. They anticipate the coming of a Redeemer who would usher in an age of righteousness the Law could never achieve.

When we get to the New Testament books, we see the promises of the Old Testament fulfilled through the Person and work of Jesus Christ.

Biographical (Matthew through John): The four Gospels, each written with a unique perspective and purpose, reveal the life, death, and resurrection of the long-anticipated Savior, emphasizing Jesus Christ's full deity and true humanity as well as the price He paid for sin.

Historical (Acts): The Acts of the Apostles narrates the spread of the gospel, as well as the birth and growth of the church under the lordship of Christ and guidance of the Holy Spirit. It shows how the work of Christ continued to extend throughout the world after His ascension into heaven.

Doctrinal (Romans through Jude): These twenty-one letters or epistles, written by specially gifted apostles and prophets (including Paul, James, Peter, John, and Jude), relay theological truth applied to everyday life. They apply the person and work of Christ to practical living.

Prophetical (Revelation): Through the spectacular vision of the apostle John, the book of Revelation helps us understand what will happen in the end times—revealing how Christ will return in glory, judgment, and power.

For a graphical overview of the books of the Bible, see the charts on pages 83 and 84.

The sixty-six books of the Bible were written over a period of 1,500 years by more than forty people who came from all walks of life and wrote with diverse, unique styles. However, the teaching throughout the books is consistent regarding creation, humanity, God, Christ, the Holy Spirit, and salvation. How does this great unity amidst diversity affect your respect for the Bible?

How does the fact of the Bible's unity support the belief in its divine origin?

How should an awareness of the various types of writings in the Bible and their role in pointing forward or back to Christ affect how you read these books?

STARTING YOUR JOURNEY

As we seek to understand and trust the reliability of God's Word, we need to keep four crucial and practical doctrines in mind: *revelation*, *inspiration*, *illumination*, and *application*.

Revelation. God chose to give His truth to us—that's revelation. It's how we know God and know about Him. If God had kept silent, our souls would have never known Him or the sweet music of His Word.

But the gospel possesses something distinctive, namely, the coming of the Savior, our Lord Jesus Christ, his suffering, and the resurrection. For the beloved prophets preached in anticipation of him, but the gospel is the imperishable finished work.[6]

—Ignatius of Antioch (c. AD 110)

How do the following passages say God has revealed Himself?

Psalm 19:1; Romans 1:20

Hebrews 1:1–2 (list two)

John 1:18

2 Peter 1:20–21

If God had not revealed Himself to us in these ways, what do you think the spiritual and moral situation of humanity would be?

Inspiration. Second Timothy 3:16 states that "all Scripture is inspired by God." The Greek word for *inspired* literally means "God-breathed." God miraculously "breathed out" His inerrant written revelation while allowing the individuality, personality, and literary style of the writers to emerge in the writing (2 Peter 1:20–21).

Read 2 Timothy 3:15–17. What terms are used to describe the use of inspired Scripture for believers? What blessings do we have because of the inspired Word?

The entire Scriptures, the prophets, and the Gospels, can be clearly, unambiguously, and harmoniously understood by all, although all do not believe them.[7]

—Irenaeus of Lyons (c. AD 185)

Illumination. Illumination addresses the understanding of God's written Word. When we read and study the Scriptures, the Author is present through His Holy Spirit, who massages truth into our hearts and stirs us to action.

According to the following passages, how do we understand the truth of Scripture?

John 16:13

1 Corinthians 2:9–16

In light of these passages, what should you do before reading your Bible, attending a Bible study, or listening to Bible teaching?

Application. Application is the ability to appropriate Scripture into daily experience—*to live it*. God's truth must churn through our minds, seep into our hearts, and flow out through every area of our lives.

Read James 1:22–25. In light of your answers to the previous questions concerning inspiration and illumination, what is the ultimate purpose of understanding and believing Scripture?

____

____

____

____

____

Are there clear commands of Scripture that you need to obey today? If so, how can you be a doer of the Word rather than just a hearer? Write the actions you'll take here:

____

____

____

____

____

Depending on your current situation and needs, select one of the following activities today to incorporate into your life over the next week or so.

____Commit to read through the book of Proverbs or one of the letters of Paul, writing down any commands you need to apply to your life by the power of God's Spirit. Reading through the book may take you longer than a week, so choose a book and commit to a time frame that's manageable for you.

____Return to the questions at the beginning of this lesson. If you're having trouble answering these, spend the next week studying the information in this workbook or using the recommended resources listed in "Resources for Probing Further," section 6, "Works on the Origins and Reliability of Scripture", page 242, to help clarify your responses to these questions.

____Memorize the key passages of Scripture that teach us about its inspiration: 2 Timothy 3:15–17 and 2 Peter 2:20–21. These will be discussed further in the next lesson.

In this lesson, we've explored not only the content but the divine and human origins of Scripture. We can be confident that God's chosen means of inspiration, transmission, canonization, and translation have placed in our hands a reliable library of living truth that we can trust as a basis for our faith and practice. Though critics have assaulted the Scriptures from the beginning, we can trust that the Holy Spirit who inspired the Bible is the same Spirit who oversaw its preservation through thousands of years of history. Its perfect harmony continues to touch our hearts and change our lives.

The Bible

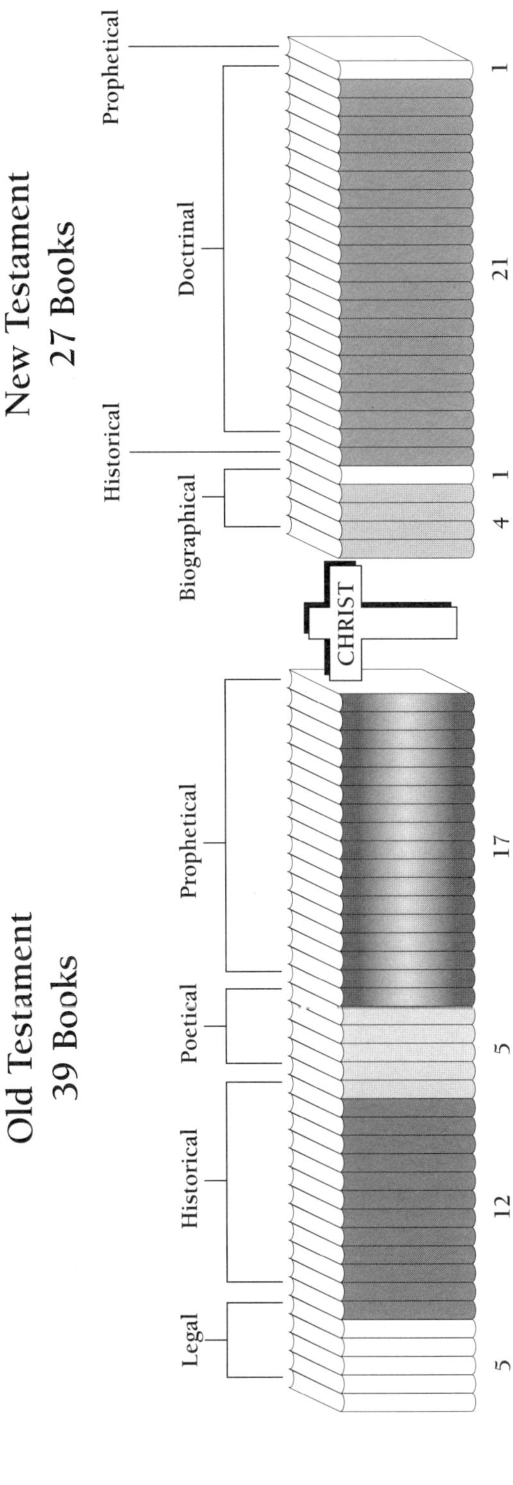
Old Testament
39 Books
Legal
5
Historical
12
Poetical
5
Prophetical
17
CHRIST
New Testament
27 Books
Biographical
4
Historical
1
Doctrinal
21
Prophetical
1

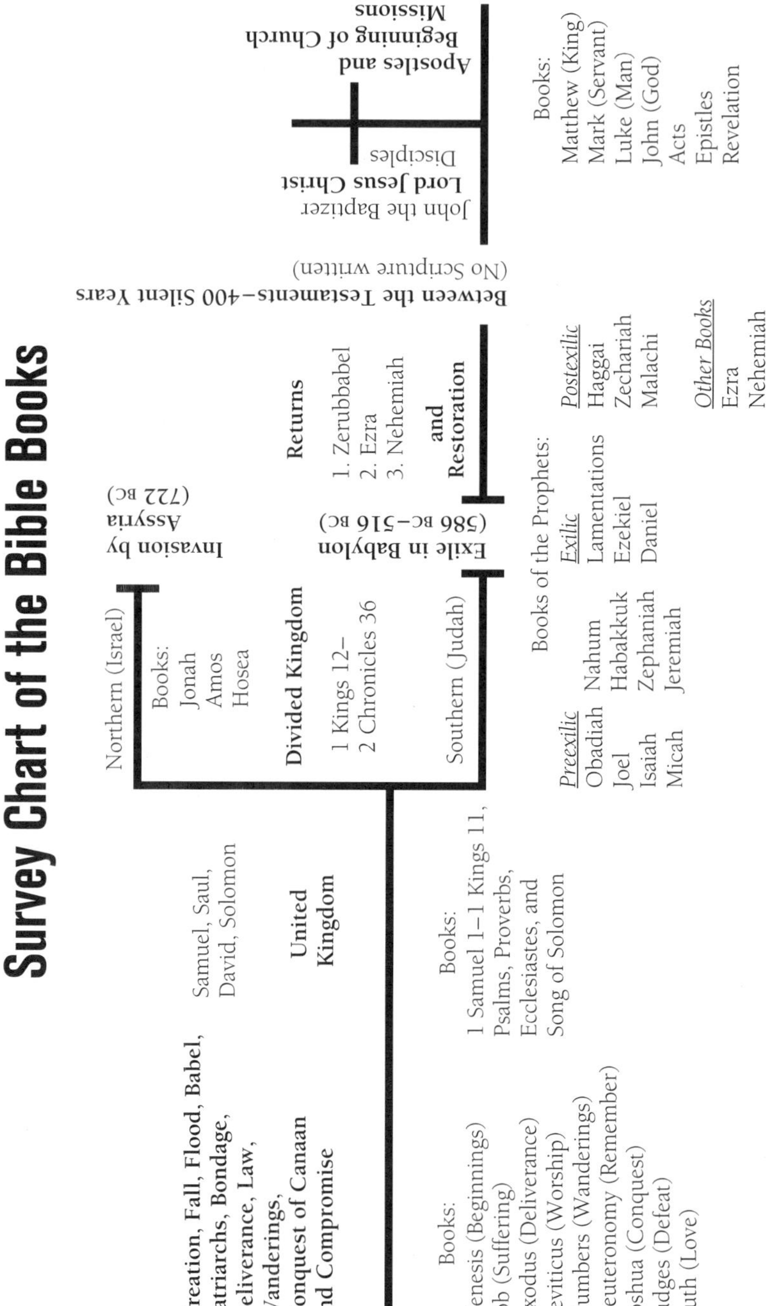
Survey Chart of the Bible Books
Creation, Fall, Flood, Babel, Patriarchs, Bondage, Deliverance, Law, Wanderings, Conquest of Canaan and Compromise
Books:
Genesis (Beginnings)
Job (Suffering)
Exodus (Deliverance)
Leviticus (Worship)
Numbers (Wanderings)
Deuteronomy (Remember)
Joshua (Conquest)
Judges (Defeat)
Ruth (Love)
Samuel, Saul, David, Solomon
United Kingdom
Books:
1 Samuel 1–1 Kings 11, Psalms, Proverbs, Ecclesiastes, and Song of Solomon
Northern (Israel)
Books:
Jonah
Amos
Hosea
Divided Kingdom
1 Kings 12–
2 Chronicles 36
Southern (Judah)
Invasion by Assyria (722 BC)
Exile in Babylon (586 BC–516 BC)
Returns
1. Zerubbabel
2. Ezra
3. Nehemiah
and Restoration
Books of the Prophets:
Preexilic
Obadiah
Joel
Isaiah
Micah
Nahum
Habakkuk
Zephaniah
Jeremiah
Exilic
Lamentations
Ezekiel
Daniel
Postexilic
Haggai
Zechariah
Malachi
Other Books
Ezra
Nehemiah
Esther
Between the Testaments—400 Silent Years
(No Scripture written)
John the Baptizer
Lord Jesus Christ
Disciples
Apostles and Beginning of Church Missions
Books:
Matthew (King)
Mark (Servant)
Luke (Man)
John (God)
Acts
Epistles
Revelation

Lesson Six

Be Sure of Your Source

2 Peter 1:12–21

THE HEART OF THE MATTER

Without a reliable source of truth, we would struggle to find our way in life, rely on shaky and sometimes illegitimate sources, and never know if we're really on the right path. It's easy in such confusion to listen to human opinion and miss God's. Because so many people these days claim to receive divine revelations from various sources, we need to be reminded of the one certain source of truth—the written Word of God.

YOU ARE HERE

Some believers volley phrases back and forth like "God told me" or "the Lord spoke to me." Usually the people who use these spiritually sounding words don't like to be quizzed on the details of exactly *how* God spoke to them. Why? Because when you look at the source of their revelation, it sometimes lacks biblical justification. When people displace the Bible as their sure source, they exchange the way of truth for a world of fiction.

Leader Help

By the end of this lesson group members should understand that the Bible is the only inerrant source of authority in the Christian life, and they should value Scripture as their guide in faith and practice.

Leader Help
Group members should consider both "natural" and "supernatural" methods of guidance that are popular today.

Other than the Bible, what might people tend to turn to for guidance in the following areas of life?

Establishing Priorities

Making Decisions regarding Relationships

Determining What's Right and Wrong

What problems have resulted in society because of reliance on these sources?

DISCOVERING THE WAY

It's not a new thing for people to grasp at both natural and supernatural means of guidance, while ignoring, adding to, or twisting God's Word. In fact, during the final days of true apostles and prophets, the warning of Paul to the Ephesians came true: "I know that after my departure savage wolves will come in among you, not sparing the flock; and from among your own selves men will arise, speaking perverse things, to draw away the disciples after them" (Acts 20:29–30). Today we have copies of these false teachers' writings—where they often claimed to have had additional special revelations from God or an elite knowledge of the secret truth. Books of the famous Nag Hammadi Library discovered in 1945, such as the Gospel of Thomas, the Gospel of Philip, and the Apocryphon of John, make up these often outlandish revelations.

Christians in the second century like Ignatius, Polycarp, Justin, and Irenaeus challenged these heretics on several counts, affirming the clear teaching of Scripture, defending the authority of the apostles' writings, and accusing their adversaries of composing fake scriptures. Today we're called to continue the work of these early heroes of the faith by discerning and defending truth.

A Personal Reminder of "The Truth"

In 2 Peter 1:1–11, Peter exhorted his readers to "be all the more diligent" in developing specific character qualities so they would be well equipped to live useful and fruitful lives for God's glory. Then, beginning in verse 12, he addressed the subject of the truth—what it is and what it's not.

Our children are being raised in a society that has largely rejected the notions of truth and morality, a society that has somewhere lost the ability to decide what is true and what is right. Truth has become a matter of taste; morality has been replaced by individual preference.[1]

—Josh McDowell

Simply stated, the truth is God's revelation, His Word. As God's children, we should establish ourselves in that truth, as Peter reminds us.

Read 2 Peter 1:12–15. Why do you think Peter felt the need to remind his readers of these important things?

In verse 15, what was the specific means Peter used to preserve his authoritative teaching after his death?

God didn't hide His truth! We don't need to search for it in the stars or try to surface it with superstitious feelings. He gave it to us in written form so that we can continually read, study, and apply it. For Peter, truth was objective—something he could leave behind with the assurance that it would provide everything necessary for the Christian life.

Based on his own experience and that of the other apostles, Peter next explained what the truth is *not*.

Read 2 Peter 1:16–18. What contrast did Peter make in verse 16?

Peter's preaching didn't rest on clever myths, as did the doctrines of the false teachers. Everything he taught concerning Christ's power and second coming came from living and learning with the Savior, whose life and teaching were confirmed by the revelation on the Mount of Transfiguration (Matthew 17:1–8). Peter could legitimately say, "God told me this," and then he could repeat the direct revelation God had given him.

What other essential Christian truths are substantiated by eyewitness accounts in these New Testament passages?

Luke 1:1–3

You have searched the Scriptures, which are true, which were given by the Holy Spirit; you know that nothing unrighteous or counterfeit is written in them.[2]

—Clement of Rome (c. AD 95)

John 19:32–36

Acts 1:21–22

1 John 1:1–2

Why is firsthand knowledge important in a defense of the Christian faith against critics and non-Christians?

DIGGING DEEPER
Where Did the Bible Come From?

How did our Bible come to us in its current form? The authentic, inspired writings of the apostles and prophets formed a unified whole through a process of *inspiration*, *transmission*, and *translation*. Charles Ryrie defined inspiration this way: "God superintended the human authors of the Bible so that they composed and recorded without error His message to mankind in the words of their original writings."[3]

Because papyrus breaks down with use, documents in the ancient world didn't last as long as they do now. To preserve a written document, a person had to copy it by hand, thus the stage of *transmission*. Those who copied Scripture were usually "scribes"—well-educated men of God who were extremely meticulous in their craft. Although minor errors in spelling and word placement may have crept in to copies of documents here and there, a comparison of all the copies we have available of a given book makes it rather easy to determine what the original writing said.

Finally, because the Old Testament was written in Hebrew or Aramaic and the New Testament was written in Greek, these books have been translated over the centuries into languages people all over the world can understand. Though they are mostly based on

Continued on next page

Continued from previous page

the same documents, the various translations of the Bible we have today differ from each other to some degree due to philosophy of translation (literal or paraphrase) or to scholars' positions regarding the definitions and translations of words. However, major, modern translations, including the New American Standard Bible, faithfully render the original meaning and notify readers of alternate translations.[4]

General Statements regarding Scripture

Recalling his unforgettable experience on the Mount of Transfiguration, Peter was prompted to give some helpful assurances concerning God's truth. The audible, firsthand revelation Peter had received gave him even further confidence in the written words handed down by the Old Testament prophets.

Read 2 Peter 1:19. The "prophetic word" here refers to all Scripture, not just the books or passages specifically dealing with future events. How did Peter counsel his readers to treat Old Testament Scripture?

For how long were they to do this?

Peter was telling his audience (and us!) to pay attention to the Scriptures with all diligence, until the day Jesus returns.[5] Think about the analogy he used. If you were to walk into a dark room, could you ignore the light coming from a lamp? Would you think it was insignificant or irrelevant to you? How vital is that light to dispelling darkness! How essential it is to everything that happens in that otherwise dark room!

In verse 20, Peter goes on to say, "But know this first of all, that no prophecy of Scripture is a matter of one's own interpretation." This statement has been understood in different ways. On one hand, it may mean that because of the inspired nature of Scripture, no writing is to be understood apart from the rest of revealed Scripture; in other words, passages must be understood in light of the whole work. Another possibility that ties in with verse 21 is that all Scripture originated with God, not with the private understanding of the authors themselves.

Take a look now at 2 Peter 1:20–21. According to verse 21, who is the ultimate Author of Scripture and responsible for its content and truthfulness?

____

____

Who is responsible for writing it down?

____

____

Unlike myths and fiction born of human authors, the Scriptures originated from God. How? They were written by men who were "inspired" or "moved" by the Holy Spirit (2 Timothy 3:16; 2 Peter 1:21). Regarding the term "moved" in 2 Peter 1:21, Kenneth Gangel writes:

> "Borne along" or "carried along" translates the word *pheromenoi*. Luke used this word in referring to a sailing vessel carried along by the wind (Acts 27:15, 17). The Scriptures' human authors were controlled by the divine Author, the Holy Spirit. Yet they were consciously involved in the process; they were neither taking dictation nor writing in a state of ecstasy.[6]

Thus, the Scriptures are inerrant. Truly, they are God's revealed written Word. In contrast, the forgeries, myths, and "secret sayings" to which scholars often refer today as the "Lost Scriptures" or "rejected gospels" fail on all accounts. They were written much later than accepted Scripture; they were not written by eyewitnesses; and they were not inspired by God.

TRUTH OR FICTION?
Are There Lost Scriptures?

Some conspiracy theorists, fiction-writers, filmmakers, and revisionist historians would like us to believe that the books we have in our New Testament were selected by prejudiced or ignorant church leaders from among hundreds of competing gospels, letters, and other Christian writings that were just as good—if not better—representations of Christianity. These people often claim that the biblical books were selected to support one group's theology, and that if other books would have been chosen, Christianity today would be completely different—more diverse and tolerant.[7] However, the truth is that the earliest Christians knew which writings of the New Testament were authentic early writings, penned by apostles or their followers, containing true accounts and doctrines of the Christian faith (see "Truth or Fiction?" on pages 72–73).

What, then, can we say of the so-called "lost books" like the Gnostic Nag Hammadi writings? These are all later books written by heretical sects or false teachers, often forgeries that were falsely attributed to apostles who had been long dead by the time the books were written. Even non-Christian scholars admit that the New Testament books we have in the Bible are the earliest and most authentic Christian writings available, and that *all* of the so-called "lost scriptures" are later, inauthentic writings that present doctrines at odds with the biblical view of Jesus. The strange—even bizarre—stories contained in these writings certainly fall under the category of "cleverly devised tales," as Peter called them in 2 Peter 1:16. If you were to pick up a copy of these "lost writings," you'd instantly recognize that the accounts are decorated with far-fetched myths and legends.

If we rely on sources other than Scripture for truth, we are casting our lives upon a sea of uncertainty. Feelings, circumstances, stars, visions, dreams—these all fluctuate. And to trust in them is to open ourselves to being seriously deluded and led into error. God's written Word, however, never changes and, when properly understood and applied, will never lead anyone into error.

STARTING YOUR JOURNEY

Like Jesus Christ, the living Word who became flesh (John 1:14), the written Word is a sure and authoritative source of truth—and it has both a divine nature and a human nature simultaneously. No wonder Satan is so determined to create doubts about Scripture and to try to displace it as our final authority in faith and practice. And no wonder Peter and the early defenders of the faith—as well as today's champions of the faith—are so determined to demonstrate its dependability. Like Peter, we also want to stir you up by way of reminder so that you may be able to call to mind two important truths at any moment, especially when you encounter opposition.

First, when you turn to God's Word, you're consulting the most reliable of all sources. Critics have long been creating doubts in the minds of many, questioning this or that passage, mocking the miraculous, and laughing at the Bible stories. All the while, they hold above Scripture their own limited knowledge, their presuppositions about what's possible, their own prejudices against absolute truth, or their desire to remain involved in a sinful lifestyle.

Second, when you make other sources—experiences, education, science, or your emotions—equal to or more reliable than the Scriptures, you'll soon fall into error. All of these other sources of information may help you better understand the truth of Scripture, but they should not replace Scripture or stand in judgment over it. Nothing can correct the Bible; rather, the Bible possesses the authority to correct all things.

To apply these reminders to your life, select one of the following activities or come up with personal applications that will reinforce your understanding about Scripture itself and the arguments for its reliability. If you chose to read a book or start a Bible-study program in lesson 5, choose something this week that allows you to realistically continue that commitment.

____Read a book on the inerrancy and reliability of Scripture from "Resources for Probing Further," section 6, "Works on the Origins and Reliability of Scripture," page 242.

____The best way to gain appreciation for and confidence in the Bible as God's unerring Word is simply to read it, study it, and apply it for yourself. If you're not already doing so, begin a systematic Bible-reading plan and study of Scripture today. Several Bible-reading plans are already available, and books on personal Bible study can prove enriching.

____ If you've been relying on other sources of authority that may be out of line with the Bible, identify them and make a decision in prayer to turn from these sources back to the Bible. Write your prayer below.

____

____

____

____

____

____ If you're having nagging doubts about the Bible's reliability, don't hide them. Find one or two people in your church who can help, or locate a reliable ministry that specializes in providing resources to answer your questions. You can locate some useful resources at **www.insight.org** or contact our Pastoral Ministries department by calling the Insight for Living Care Line at 972-473-5097 (8 A.M. to 5 P.M. Central Time) or by writing: Insight for Living, Pastoral Ministries Department, Post Office Box 269000, Plano, Texas 75026-9000.

In this lesson we discovered that the Bible is the only inerrant source of authority in the Christian life—the only reliable guide in faith and practice. While we may use other sources of information and learning to supplement our understanding of Scripture, the Bible is the only source that can never be corrected. No so-called "lost gospel" or "missing Scripture" can hold a candle to the eyewitness accounts, inspired teachings, and infallible record of God's redemptive plan for humanity as revealed through the Word and works of Jesus Christ.

Lesson Seven

Jesus: His Existence before Creation

Selected Scriptures

THE HEART OF THE MATTER

Is Jesus of Nazareth the eternal God or did His life begin in a manger? Is it true that Jesus is coeternal with the Father? Was He existent in eternity long before the creation of the world? How could He be both God and man if He always existed? These questions touch on some of the most central issues of Christianity. The truth that Jesus of Nazareth is fully divine unravels all the revisionist history and fantastic fiction created and supported by unbelievers.

Leader Help
By the end of this lesson group members should understand that the deity of Christ is a vital doctrine of the Christian faith, recognize biblical support for the doctrine, and feel confident in its truth and application.

YOU ARE HERE

C. S. Lewis, author of the classic children's series, *The Chronicles of Narnia*, began his academic career at Oxford as a brilliant and confident young atheist. As a boy of ten, Lewis had watched his mother die of cancer while a silent God seemed to ignore his desperate prayers to save her. In the years that followed, Lewis dismissed the existence of a caring, loving God and relegated the Bible to storybook status. As a student, his atheism flowered in Oxford's soil. But slowly and certainly God was uprooting him to shake him free. In his autobiographical book, *Surprised by Joy*, Lewis described his eventual surrender after years of God's pursuit of his soul.

> You must picture me alone in that room in Magdalen, night after night, feeling, whenever my mind lifted even for a second from my work, the steady, unrelenting approach of Him whom I so earnestly desired not to meet. That which I greatly feared had at last come upon me. In the Trinity Term of 1929 I gave in, and admitted that God was God, and knelt and prayed: perhaps, that night, the most dejected and reluctant convert in all England. I did not then see what is now the most shining and obvious thing; the Divine humility which will accept a convert even on such terms. The Prodigal Son at least walked home on his own feet. But who can duly adore that Love which will open the high gates to a prodigal who is brought in kicking, struggling, resentful, and darting his eyes in every direction for a chance of escape?[1]

On that night, C. S. Lewis met Jesus and knew the truth about who Jesus was: his Savior and Lord.

Read Jesus's question and the disciples' answers in Mark 8:27–29. Today, who do both Christians and non-Christians often say Jesus is or was?

Who do you say Jesus is? Why?

DISCOVERING THE WAY

Upon entering Caesarea Philippi, Jesus penetrated His disciples' thinking with this question: "Who do people say that the Son of Man is?" (Matthew 16:13). It echoes as loudly today as it did back then. It was a question whose answer brought C. S. Lewis from the darkness of atheism into the light of Christianity. And it's a question every believer must be ready to answer.

Leader Help

These questions are meant to surface the *variety* of answers to this question of who Jesus was and is—both outside the Christian faith and even among believers. At this point, do not be too concerned about finding the *right* answer. It will become more clear as we work through the next few lessons.

Leader Help

Depending on the makeup of your group, you might want to look more closely at the charge that the early Christians fabricated legends and myths about Christ because this is a common assertion made by unbelieving historians. Read the "Digging Deeper" feature, "The Reliability of the Apostles' Reports" beginning on this page. Then, lead your group to consider these questions: Based on Luke 1:1–4; 1 Corinthians 9:1; 15:3–8; 2 Peter 1:16; and 1 John 1:1–3, why is it difficult to believe that the stories about Jesus are legends and myths? Could people who made up myths and legends write such words? What would we call these writers if their description of events were only myths or legends?

The Question of Jesus's Identity

As you discovered at the beginning of this lesson, people today have all sorts of opinions about who Jesus was and is:

- A great human teacher
- The founder of Christianity
- A carpenter's son from Nazareth
- A Jew who claimed to be the Messiah
- A first-century martyr who died for a noble cause
- A figment of the disciples' imagination

DIGGING DEEPER

The Reliability of the Apostles' Reports

In his book *Mere Christianity*, C. S. Lewis narrowed the options regarding Jesus's identity to three: a liar, a lunatic, or the Lord.[2] Today, another category has become increasingly popular among historians—*legend*. Some say the real, historical Jesus never claimed to be anything more than a rabbi who preached the coming judgment of God. After Jesus's death, His disciples and other followers constructed stories and myths about Him. These historians teach that the "Christ of faith" is really fiction while the "Jesus of history" was just a normal human. We all have to make the same choice about Jesus from these four options—was He a liar, a lunatic, a legend, or the Lord?

In the end, believers must rely on the credibility of eyewitnesses who performed miracles as a sign of their divine authority (Mark 16:20; Hebrews 2:3–4). In fact, Paul reminded the Corinthians, "The signs of a true apostle were performed among you with all perseverance, by signs and wonders and miracles" (2 Corinthians 12:12; also Romans 15:18–19). If Paul had not really performed these signs to confirm his authority and the truthfulness of his message, could he have claimed in a letter that he had? Of course not. His audience would have known better, and he would have lost all credibility. Therefore, we must decide whether to trust the eyewitness testimony of the first-century apostles who gave their lives for their faith or the remote skepticism of twenty-first century scholars who make their livelihood by selling books that attack the faith.

Jesus said to Thomas when he confessed Christ as Lord and God, "Because you have seen Me, have you believed? Blessed are they who did not see, and yet believed" (John 20:29). Perhaps reflecting on Jesus's words to Thomas years earlier, Peter made a similar statement: "Though you have not seen Him, you love Him, and though you do not see Him now, but believe in Him, you greatly rejoice with joy inexpressible and full of glory" (1 Peter 1:8).

Continued on next page

Continued from previous page

We do not believe in the deity of Christ blindly, nor do we believe fanciful tales by self-serving "witnesses." We rely on the testimony of witnesses who are reliable. We trust the writings of believers who are trustworthy.

Who did people say that Jesus was during His earthly ministry? The scribes and Pharisees' messianic expectations were challenged by this unsettling preacher from Nazareth: "Who is this man who speaks blasphemies?" (Luke 5:21); "Who is this man who even forgives sins?" (Luke 7:49). King Herod pondered: "Who is this man about whom I hear such things?" (Luke 9:9). Finally, Pontius Pilate asked Jesus, "Are you the King of the Jews?" (Luke 23:3).

The Jewish rabbis and scribes had a variety of expectations about what the Messiah would be like and what He would do when He came, but their picture was unclear. While God had revealed many clues about the Messiah throughout the Old Testament, many Jews overlooked them or failed to connect them to Jesus.

Consider the following Old Testament prophecies about the Messiah. In light of the corresponding New Testament passages, what do they tell us about Jesus?

Psalm 45:6–7 and Hebrews 1:8–9

Isaiah 7:14 and Matthew 1:23

Isaiah 9:6 and Titus 2:13

Zechariah 2:10–11 and John 12:45

This is he who was from the beginning, who appeared as new yet proved to be old. . . . This is the Eternal One, who today is accounted a Son.[3]

—The Epistle to Diognetus (c. AD 150)

How do these passages predict a coming Messiah who would be not merely human but also divine? Give specific examples.

We've learned that doubters in the first century had many expectations for who the Messiah would be; they also held many views regarding Jesus's identity. But who did Jesus claim to be? When Jesus asked His disciples who they believed Him to be, Peter's classic answer resounded through the corridors of history: "You are the Christ, the Son of the living God" (Matthew 16:16). Thomas makes a similar confession in John 20:28, where He said to Jesus, "My Lord and my God!"[4]

TRUTH OR FICTION?
Did Constantine Declare Jesus to be "God" in AD 325?

The Da Vinci Code is not alone in claiming that in the fourth century, the Emperor Constantine changed Christianity to further his political agenda. Historians or false teachers who deny Christ's deity sometimes suggest this event as a possibility.

The truth is, Christians regarded Jesus as both God *and* man from the very beginning.

In John 1:1, 14, we see that the eternal Son of God (the Word) was called "God," and at the moment of His miraculous conception, He took on full humanity—including a body of material flesh. Repeatedly in the New Testament, Jesus is declared both man and God (John 1:1, 14; Romans 1:3; Galatians 4:4; Colossians 2:9; Philippians 2:6–8; and 1 Timothy 3:16). The idea that later Christians selected or changed Scripture to downplay Christ's humanity in favor of divinity is complete fiction. In fact, Christians in the first and second centuries had to *defend* Christ's full humanity against heretics like the Gnostics who argued that Christ was *only* God but not really human (1 John 4:2; 2 John 1:7).

Beyond the New Testament, followers of the apostles continued to emphasize that Jesus is both God *and* man at the same time. Ignatius, the pastor of Antioch who was martyred in about AD 110 and who may have known the apostle John, wrote: "There is only one physician, who is both flesh and spirit, born and unborn, God in man, true life in death, both from Mary and from God, first subject to suffering and then beyond it, Jesus Christ our Lord."[5] Ignatius also deliberately called Jesus "God" several times in his writings.

The claim that Jesus was regarded by early Christians as only a great man until later Christians emphasized His divinity is untrue.

Continued on next page

I praise you, I bless you, I glorify you, through the eternal and heavenly High Priest, Jesus Christ, your beloved Son, through whom to you with him and the Holy Spirit be glory both now and for the ages to come. Amen.[6]

—Polycarp of Smyrna (c. AD 155)

Continued from previous page

In fact, the central claim of Christianity has always been that the eternal, divine Son willingly became fully human for us, lived a perfect life, died a brutal death to pay for our sins, and rose again as the victorious God-man, who will come again in judgment. This truth has stood against false teachers from the age of the apostles to our own day, and it will stand as truth for all generations to come.

The Issue of Jesus's Eternality

Jesus Himself claimed to be God and to have existed eternally with the Father before adding true humanity to His deity. This issue became a major point of contention with Jewish leaders. Although prophecies in the Old Testament indicated that the Messiah would be divine (Isaiah 9:6), the idea of a Trinity within the unity of God was unthinkable to many Jews. It should come as no surprise, then, that when Jesus made statements that suggested His eternality *and* deity, they were met with stiff resistance.

Read John 5:15–18; 8:52–59; and 10:30–33. Consider each of these conflicts between Jesus and the Jewish teachers. Why were they so angry with Jesus?

___

___

___

___

Why was this such a stumbling block for them?

GETTING TO THE ROOT

In John 8:58, when Jesus referred to Himself as "I am," He was not only asserting His supremacy over Abraham and over time, He was also asserting His eternality and deity. In Greek the phrase is *egō eimi*, which corresponds with God's name in Exodus 3:14, "I am who I am." In John 8:58, Jesus used a completely unexpected and inappropriate verb tense for somebody who wanted to simply say He existed before Abraham. He could have said, "Before Abraham was, I was" (or "I have been"). Instead, he used the present tense, intentionally reminding His challengers of the name of God—the "I am" who is not merely *before* all things, but outside the confines of past, present, and future.

The eternality and deity of Christ was asserted not only by Jesus Himself but also by His closest disciples, John and Peter, and the great missionary to the Gentiles, Paul.

Read John 1:1–3, 14, 18. In these verses, how are God the Father and the Word (the Son) distinguished?

How do these verses equate the Father and the Son?

According to verse 3, why couldn't the Word be part of creation?

According to verse 18, what is the only way we can know the Father?

In the following passages, how is Christ's relationship to deity described?

Philippians 2:5–7

Colossians 1:16–17

Colossians 2:8–9

Leader Help

Though these passages are optional for group study, they demonstrate that the eternality and deity of Christ are not just John's ideas but the common teaching of Christians from the beginning. You may want to prepare answers to these questions beforehand and briefly share them with the group.

Titus 2:13

____

____

____

Hebrews 1:8–9

____

____

____

2 Peter 1:17

____

____

____

How are these statements about Christ's relationship to God the Father and to creation similar to the statements made by John (John 1:1–3, 14, 18)?

____

____

____

____

____

STARTING YOUR JOURNEY

We have spent considerable time reaffirming Jesus's true divinity and eternality. Obviously, we believe that this doctrine is crucial. In fact, the deity of Jesus Christ is important on two levels, theological and practical.

Theologically, if Jesus is not eternally God, then the credibility of all of Christianity is undermined. The identification of Jesus as Lord (God) stands at the heart of Christian theology. Scripture clearly affirms it. The church has consistently declared it from the beginning. Jesus as the God-man is an essential truth of the Christian faith. If this isn't true, then the New Testament isn't true and neither is Christianity.

Practically, if Jesus was just a mere man, our faith is empty and our hope vanishes. We couldn't turn to Him for salvation from our sins or for help in our day-to-day struggles, because He would have only the same human power and resources that we have.

Considering the vital theological and practical implications of the true deity of Christ, select one of the following activities to pursue this week.

____Memorize key Scriptures that address Christ's deity. Select from the following: John 1:1–3; John 20:28; Colossians 1:16–17; Colossians 2:8–9; or Hebrews 1:8–9.

____Read one or more of the four Gospels, and note all of the places where Jesus asserts His deity either in His words or actions.

____Read one of the resources from "Resources for Probing Further," section 7, "Biblical, Historical, and Theological Treatments of Christ's Person and Work," page 243.

____Spend some time studying the chart, "Liar, Lunatic, Legend, or Lord?" on the next page. If possible, try to memorize the various options and arguments in each branch to better organize your own thoughts on this matter and to be equipped to handle objections from others.

In this lesson we learned that the essential doctrine of the eternal existence and deity of Christ is taught clearly in Scripture by the eyewitnesses of His resurrection and those who knew Him best. These earliest disciples literally gave their lives for this truth—some by brutal torture. Through the suggested activities at the end of the lesson, you should be equipped to respond to the common challenges of Christ's deity. It really boils down to four options—either He's a mere legend, a liar, a lunatic, or the Lord God.

Liar, Lunatic, Legend, or Lord?

The Bible says Jesus claimed to be God

John 5:15–18; 8:58; 10:30

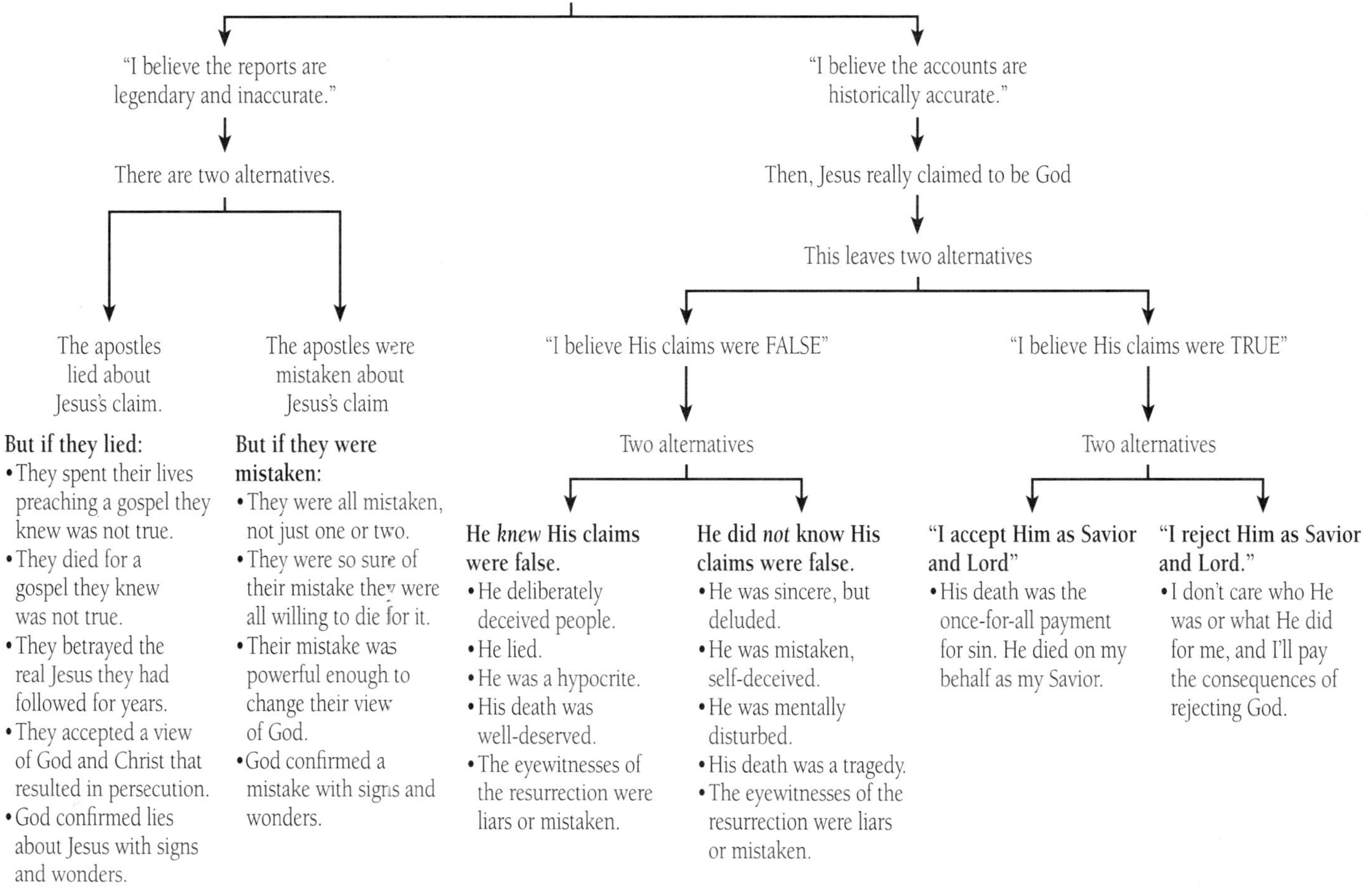

 This diagram is adapted from a chart in Josh McDowell, *The New Evidence That Demands a Verdict* (Nashville: Thomas Nelson, 1999), 158, which was based on the ideas of C. S. Lewis, *Mere Christianity*, 55–57. Material supplemented by the Creative Ministries department of Insight for Living.

Lesson Eight

Jesus: A Birth like None Other

Luke 1:26 – 35; Matthew 1:18 –25

THE HEART OF THE MATTER

The cries of that baby in a manger were the first audible sounds of God's voice from a human mouth . . . but only a few were listening. Few expected the arrival of the God-man, especially not in a stable at Bethlehem. Even today, many regard the lowly birth of the Son of God as a fairy tale. But if we return to Bethlehem for a moment, we can stand in awe at the sight of the eternal Son of God who became a man.

YOU ARE HERE

In our society, when the rich and famous marry, newspapers, magazines, and television newscasts announce it to the world. When a film star has a child, the paparazzi sneak photos of the new Hollywood royalty to sell to the highest bidder. Images of coronations, royal weddings, presidential inaugurations, and even papal visits draw massive crowds of people who want to catch even a glimpse of the event.

Leader Help

By the end of this lesson, group members should understand the necessity of the virgin birth and sinless humanity of Jesus Christ in Christian theology and value the importance of this doctrine for salvation and Christian living.

Describe a recent celebrity event such as a marriage, birth, coronation, or inauguration that drew a lot of world attention. Who attended the event? How was it celebrated? Who was interested?

____

____

____

____

____

Why do you think the rich, famous, and powerful hold events this way? What do they communicate about themselves?

____

____

____

____

____

What would it communicate if these same famous people decided to have quiet, inexpensive celebrations instead? How do you think this would be interpreted or received by the public?

____

____

____

____

____

In light of typical celebrity fanfare, the biblical account of the birth of the eternal Son of God is startling. The only available accommodation for the expectant couple was a stable crowded with the animals of the inn's guests. A feeding trough stuffed with hay became a crib. Sheep, donkeys, and furtive barn mice were the Heir's only attendants. A barnyard stench hung heavy in the air—a disquieting place for a woman in the throes of childbirth. Of course, there were countless rejoicing angels announcing His arrival—but only to a lowly band of blue-collar shepherds.

And thus, in the little town of Bethlehem on that one silent night, the royal birth of God's only Son tiptoed quietly by while the rest of the world slept.

Not quite what you would expect of a royal birth, was it?

Now the virginity of Mary and her giving birth were hidden from the ruler of this age, as was also the death of the Lord—three mysteries to be loudly proclaimed, yet which were accomplished in the silence of God. . . . Consequently all magic and every kind of spell were dissolved, the ignorance so characteristic of wickedness vanished, and the ancient kingdom was abolished, when God appeared in human form to bring the newness of eternal life.[1]

—Ignatius of Antioch (c. AD 110)

DISCOVERING THE WAY

Without Jesus in the manger, Christianity cannot exist. Apart from the real birth of the eternal Son of God, Christianity is just an empty feeding trough of wood and straw. Jesus Christ and Christianity are really one and the same, and Christians—those called by Christ's name—are personally related to Him.

However, just as it is easy to lose the simplicity and purity of Christmas amidst the ribbons and bows of the holidays, so it is easy to lose our devotion to Christ amid the tinsel and glitter of life.

Read 2 Corinthians 11:2–4. According to this passage, what is Paul's fear?

____

____

____

____

____

According to verse 4, what three issues distracted Paul's readers from the simplicity of their devotion to Christ?

____

____

____

____

____

The Superiority of Jesus Christ

Not only is Christ central, He is also superior to everything in heaven and on earth. He is not only man, He is God. His birth was no ordinary birth; it was a sinless arrival.

As you may recall from the previous lesson, the Son of God has always existed (John 8:58). Before the earth was created, Jesus existed as God alongside God the Father (John 1:1). Jesus is superior to all because He is Creator of all (John 1:3). Jesus—who is the same yesterday, today, and forever (Hebrews 13:8)—was, is, and forever will be God. Yet from the moment the eternal Son of God took on true human life in the womb of Mary (John 1:14), He was also fully man—the God-man.

DIGGING DEEPER

The Necessity of the Virgin Birth

How could God become human yet remain uninfected by the sinfulness of humanity that all people inherit from Adam (Romans 5:12, 14; 1 Corinthians 15:22)? After all, a savior couldn't *really* be a savior if he were contaminated by sin like we are. His birth and life would have to be unique to preserve him from the inheritance of the sin and guilt transmitted to all of Adam's descendants. How could God accomplish this?

As a first option, God could have chosen for Jesus to have been born of a *good* human father and mother. However, as David described, all humans conceived naturally by a father and mother are "brought forth in iniquity" (Psalm 51:5, 58:3; Romans 5:12). In this option, Jesus would have been completely human but not divine. This was the second-century heresy of the Ebionites, who rejected the virgin birth and deity of Christ.

As a second option, God could have chosen His Son to be created, like an angel, having neither father nor mother. As a created being, He would have been preserved from sin's contamination. In this case, however, He would have been completely divine but not really human. This heresy was asserted by the Docetists, who taught that Christ took on only the *appearance* of a man but was not really born of a woman at all.

As a third option, God could have chosen to indwell a real human being, Jesus, by the spirit of the Son, sort of like a demon-possessed person in the Bible (Matthew 12:43–45). But this would have produced two separate persons—the divine Son could have entered and left the body of Jesus as He pleased. This theory was the error of the Adoptionists, who taught that the divine Christ inhabited the body of the human Jesus.

As a final option, God could have chosen to select a virgin who, through miraculous conception, could give birth to a child both fully human and fully divine. *And this is what He did*, as the multiple testimonies in Scripture attest (Luke 1:26–35; Matthew 1:18).

Prophecies of the Incarnation

About eight hundred years before Christ's birth, the prophet Isaiah prophesied of this special event—the virgin birth and coming of God as a man to live among humans. Let's take a closer look at two of these prophecies and the ways they were fulfilled in the New Testament.

Read Isaiah 7:14, then Matthew 1:18–25. How did Matthew tell us the prophecy of Isaiah was fulfilled?

Use three words to describe Joseph's emotions when he was told what would happen to Mary.

Read Isaiah 9:6–7. then Luke 1:26–35. How did Luke tell us the prophecy of Isaiah was fulfilled?

Use three words to describe Mary's emotions when she was told what would happen to her.

Why do you think Mary and Joseph reacted the way they did to the angel's news? How does this differ from those today who doubt the virgin birth?

How do you think Matthew and Luke received their information about Mary and Joseph and the birth of Jesus? (Hint: Luke 1:1–3.)

Leader Help

Encourage your group to look back through the Old Testament prophecies examined on page 126, and work together to provide a wide variety of answers to the question on this page. Be sure to include appropriate Scripture references—these will be very important for your group as they discuss these issues in the future.

How might we use the Old Testament prophecies of the coming Messiah to help skeptics today understand and accept the uniqueness of Jesus Christ? Be specific.

____

____

____

____

____

GETTING TO THE ROOT

In Isaiah 7:14, the Hebrew word for "virgin," *almah*, simply referred to a "young woman" or maiden.[2] When the Hebrew Old Testament was translated into Greek, the translators used the word *parthenos*, the technical term for a woman who had not known a man intimately.[3] This word choice reflected the uniqueness of the Messiah's coming—as well as the means God chose to make this special person truly "Immanuel"—"God with us" (Matthew 1:23).

STARTING YOUR JOURNEY

You may not realize it, but the virgin birth has far-reaching ramifications. Because Christianity centers on the person of Christ, if Christ were only a man and not the perfect God-man, then Christianity would fall apart in at least three areas.

First, a natural savior provides no supernatural help. We need supernatural forgiveness because we have a lifetime of sins and regrets that cannot be forgiven or relieved by natural means. And we need the supernatural promise of eternal life because we are helpless in ourselves to conquer our greatest fear, death. On the other hand, if the Son had never become truly human, He could not have died for our sins. His sacrifice could be payment for our sins, specifically because he was fully, but sinlessly, human. For salvation to be effective, Jesus had to be both God *and* man.

Second, a strictly human savior offers no divine hope. When we would hurt, we'd receive only a temporary hug. When we would need forgiveness, we'd see only a condescending smile. We'd have no hope that is grounded in a reality bigger than our own. His divinity allows for the transcendence of His mercy and grace. On the other hand, His humanity creates the depth of His understanding. If the Son had not become man, He would not have met us where we are, empathizing with our suffering and knowing our pain firsthand (Hebrews 4:14–16).

For he was born a son,
and led as a lamb,
and slaughtered as a
sheep,
and buried as a man,
and rose from the dead
as God,
being God by his nature
and a man.[4]

—Melito of Sardis
(c. AD 165)

And third, a sinful savior is really no savior at all. If your only hope of rescue is the person sinking in quicksand next to you, then you have no hope. A savior must be sinless, free from that which enslaves us (John 8:34). We have just such a Savior in Christ because His birth was truly like none other. On the other hand, if the Son had not become a man, He could not have fulfilled the Law and overcome sin and death for us (Galatians 4:3–5). Again, Jesus had to be both God *and* man.

In summary, what are the practical implications of the virgin birth? Simply put, if the divine Son of God had not become a sinless man, we would still be dead in our sins, and no human would ever receive forgiveness and eternal life. Besides that, believers would never have the blessings of salvation—spiritual gifts, answered prayer, divine guidance and provision, or empowerment to conquer sin.

Spend the next week re-centering your life on the "simplicity and purity of devotion to Christ" (2 Corinthians 11:3). In your daily time with the Lord and His Word, reflect on each of the following thoughts, pondering the Scripture passages as they relate to the person of Jesus Christ. You may want to write prayers, compose poetry, journal, memorize the Scriptures, or discuss your thoughts with others.

____God sent His Son from heaven to redeem humanity. In the same way, God sends His Spirit to convict unbelievers about the truth of His Son, calling them to salvation. Reflect on Galatians 4:3–7, considering how this passage relates our salvation to the coming of the Son of God as a sinless man. Are you certain of your own adoption as an heir of God through Jesus Christ? Would you be able to share the good news of salvation clearly to others? You may want to read the "How to Begin a Relationship with God" section at the end of this workbook. It clearly explains Jesus Christ's payment for our sin and how sinners can be forgiven.

____Our supernatural Savior, conceived by the power of the Holy Spirit and born miraculously of a virgin, promised that He is ready and willing to lavish the riches of His grace on us. By His humanity, He has been able to identify with us and pay the price for our sins. By His deity, He is able to keep His promises and give us eternal life. Reflect on Ephesians 1:3–23, carefully considering the blessings you have because of Christ's person and work.

____When you wrestle with difficult circumstances or struggle in relationships beyond your ability to resolve, how do you really view God's attitude toward the situation? Do you view Him as someone who will ultimately "deliver [you] from all [your] fears" (Psalm 34:4) or as someone who "helps those who help themselves"? Reflect on Hebrews 4:14–16, as you ponder how Christ's coming in the flesh should influence how you view God's help in difficult times.

This lesson emphasized the necessity of the virgin birth and true deity and humanity of Christ. These are not just matters of doctrine or theology, but they make up the central truth of the Christian faith. If Jesus did not become incarnate by the Virgin Mary, He would be unable to pay for your sins. There's nothing impractical or theoretical about it. Your understanding of Jesus Christ's humanity and divinity will directly affect how you relate to Him.

Lesson Nine

Jesus: His God-Man Lifestyle

Selected Scriptures

THE HEART OF THE MATTER

If Jesus is the eternal Son of God who became the sinless Son of Man by a virgin birth, then He is superior to all others not only in His person but also in His works. In His incarnation, the Son added true humanity to His true divinity, resulting in two natures in one extraordinary person—the God-man. A serious examination of the life of Jesus of Nazareth must include a deep reflection on the nature of His person. If Jesus is fully God and fully man, as He claimed to be, then all human history must be understood in light of this truth—and any who choose to reject Jesus Christ are rejecting the God who made them.

Leader Help

By the end of this lesson, group members should be able to define the doctrine of the incarnation of Jesus Christ and understand the biblical support for it, as well as express its practical implications and application for salvation.

YOU ARE HERE

Our primary sources for learning and understanding the words and deeds of Jesus are the four canonical Gospels—Matthew, Mark, Luke, and John. Though each one wrote from a unique perspective and to a unique audience, they all present a unified portrait of Jesus—perfect man and perfect God. Naturally, unbelieving historians and skeptical scholars attack the reliability of these historical documents, regarding them as fictitious, legendary, or mythical accounts that give us little insight into the real, historical Jesus (whom they regard as merely a man who lived and died in the first century).

These scholars try to point out contradictions in the various "Christs" portrayed in the Gospels and cast doubts on their reports. They add other "lost gospels" like The Gospel of Thomas or The Gospel of Philip to complicate further the picture of Jesus. Or groups like the Jesus Seminar—in their relentless quest for the "historical" Jesus—remove material from the Gospels to create a Jesus who fits their historical and religious presuppositions. These attacks on the Gospels' picture of Jesus Christ as fully God and fully man—as evidenced by His words and works—are certainly not new. The Gospels have been attacked by unbelievers from the very beginning. Today, however, these scholars have a much greater voice through mass media, and their voices are being heard and believed by many.

How would you respond to each of these typical charges of those who don't believe that Christ is the God-man?

"The Gospels contradict themselves. In one place they say Jesus is a man who eats, sleeps, weeps, and bleeds. In another it says he's a god who can walk on water, perform miracles, and know the unknowable. How could both of those be true?"

"Jesus's earliest disciples didn't believe he was God. Just read the Gospels—they emphasize Jesus's humanity, not his deity. When they talk about him being 'divine' or 'like God,' it's more a quality of his humanity—like the 'divine' in all of us. Jesus epitomized the great potential of humankind."

Leader Help

Consider the following charges carefully. As your group begins to discuss them, be aware that group members may not be able to answer these questions adequately at this point. You may want to prepare a few potential answers before the group meets, using material and Scripture passages from previous lessons. Also, note that your group will have a chance to answer these charges again at the end of this lesson, after more information has been provided.

"Christians who changed and edited the Gospels wanted to downplay or delete references to Jesus's humanity. The idea that Jesus was a god gave Christianity a greater appeal to pagans. So the Gospels we have today try to conceal Jesus's humanity and reinforce his deity."

Do you feel equipped to handle these accusations against the biblical view of Christ? If not, what areas are still unclear for you?

DISCOVERING THE WAY

In the simplest terms, the doctrine of the incarnation is the union of deity and humanity in the person of Jesus Christ. This union took place at the moment of conception, when both natures united, inseparable yet unmixed (Luke 1:31–35). In this mysterious union, undiminished deity was veiled in untainted humanity. Coequal, coeternal, and coexistent with the Father, Jesus is both fully God and fully human. In the incarnation, God dived down into the depths of creation and became a man.

By now you should be familiar with the key passages for the incarnation: John 1:1 and 1:14. Considered together, these verses assert the heart of the doctrine:

> In the beginning was the Word, and the Word was with God, and the Word was God. . . . And the Word became flesh, and dwelt among us, and we saw His glory, glory as of the only begotten from the Father, full of grace and truth.

Of course, these verses are not alone in asserting the deity and humanity of Christ. However, this passage has long been regarded as the central doctrine of the person of Jesus Christ and of the Christian faith. Why? If God had not become human, we would be eternally lost.

Leader Help
You might want to break your group into smaller teams, with each team studying one of the passages on this page. Then, if possible, write each team's conclusions on a board for all to see and discuss.

The following Scripture passages assert both the deity and humanity of Jesus Christ. For each one, note the manner in which deity and humanity are mentioned and how they are related in the person of Jesus Christ.

Romans 1:3–4

2 Corinthians 5:19

Colossians 2:9

2 John 1:7

DOORWAY TO HISTORY
Creeds and Councils in the Early Church

In the early church—perhaps as early as the days of the apostles themselves—believers used creeds (or "confessions") to fulfill a dual purpose. First, creeds helped to summarize and define the cardinal doctrines of Christianity for those being instructed in the faith prior to or following baptism. The creedal formulas provided unity among all Christians, despite differences on minor issues. Second, because certain phrases in the various confessions were designed to rule out false teachings, creeds helped the church keep false doctrine from gaining ground in the assemblies. For example, the Ebionites taught that Jesus was not born of a virgin, but was the natural son of Joseph, and Gnostics taught that a lesser deity—not the almighty Father—created the material universe.

As the church continued to encounter false teachers and new questions, the creeds developed and grew, though the doctrines of the Father, Son, and Holy Spirit continued to play the central role, with the person and work of Christ always in the spotlight. The Nicene Creed (approved at the Council of Nicaea in AD 325) and the Constantinopolitan Creed (approved in AD 381) combated the errors of Arius, who denied the true deity of Christ.

Continued on next page

So, following the saintly fathers, we all with one voice teach the confession of one and the same Son, our Lord Jesus Christ: the same perfect in divinity and perfect in humanity, the same truly God and truly man, of a rational soul and a body.[1]

—The Definition of Chalcedon, AD 451

Continued from previous page

These early creeds also formed the doctrinal basis by which later teachings were determined to be heresy. The Council of Ephesus (held in AD 431) condemned the teaching of Nestorius, who divided Christ into two separate persons—one divine, the other human. The Council of Chalcedon (held in AD 451) condemned the teaching that the divine nature and human nature were mixed and blurred into a new nature, neither human nor divine. In all of these creeds and councils, the ancient doctrine of the incarnation was affirmed and defended—Jesus Christ is one person with two complete natures, human and divine, without mixture and without separation.

To this day, these creeds and councils continue to hold a place of prominence in Christian history, theology, and worship. Though not all churches and denominations pay close attention to these creeds, all true Christians agree with the basic theology expressed in them.[2]

An Explanation: Two Natures in One Person

A beautiful and breathtaking picture is found in Philippians 2:5–7. In this sacred scene, divine humility glows in the subdued light of the incarnation, bathed in hues of another world. The Creator willingly submitted to the laws of the very universe He had created. He released His independence and became dependent. He gave up being the One who is served to become the Servant.

Read Philippians 2:5–7. According to verse 6, what did the Son of God surrender?

____

____

____

What was the result of this surrender (verse 7)?

____

____

____

This passage requires an important clarification. In making "himself nothing" (Philippians 2:7), the Son did not shed His deity. In becoming a man, He did *not* become something less than God. Rather, He voluntarily left His place of glory and released His grasp on His divine prerogatives. And He did all of this *for us*. Only as a man could Jesus be tempted by Satan, fulfill the law, suffer, and die. Only as God could Jesus do all of these things *in our place*.

[The Lord Jesus Christ is] the same essence with the Father according to his divinity, and the same essence with us according to his humanity; like us in all things—except sin.[3]

—The Definition of Chalcedon, AD 451

Read Hebrews 4:14–16, and evaluate how Jesus Christ's humanity and divinity affect our relationship to Him.

____

____

____

____

____

How does the fact that Jesus is fully God and fully man affect how you can personally approach Him in prayer?

____

____

____

____

____

Some Illustrations: Both Natures Revealed

Numerous eyewitnesses cite times when deity peeked through the drawn curtain of Jesus's humanity. In the following study, we'll examine several passages that illustrate the profound humility and even fragility of His human condition, while at the same time illuminating His deity and power.

In the following selected accounts from the life of Christ, read the passage carefully, then fill in the chart, explaining how each passage illustrates Christ's deity and humanity.

Matthew 14:22–33

Deity	Humanity

Luke 8:22–25

Deity	Humanity

John 11:32–36, 41–46

Deity	Humanity

[We confess] one and the same Christ, Son, Lord, only-begotten, acknowledged in two natures which undergo no confusion, no change, no division, no separation; at no point was the difference between the natures taken away through the union.[4]

—The Definition of Chalcedon, AD 451

TRUTH OR FICTION?
Was Jesus Married?

The Da Vinci Code is not alone in its claim that Jesus of Nazareth was married and had a child. Other controversial works, like *The Last Temptation of Christ* and *Holy Blood, Holy Grail*, argue for the same version of history. Often people will appeal to Jesus's true humanity to support this view—almost all other Jewish men were married at the time, so why would Jesus be any different?

First, no early suggestion exists that says Jesus was ever married. Even the so-called proof from the Gnostic Gospel of Philip is untrue. *The Da Vinci Code* suggests that the word for "companion" in Aramaic means "spouse," but the truth is that the Gospel of Philip was written in Coptic and based on a Greek text—and the word for "companion" in both of these languages doesn't mean "spouse" but "friend."

Second, the claim that rabbis or respectable Jewish leaders *had* to be married is also false. The sect of the Essenes, for instance, emphasized celibacy. Paul recommended the single life for the sake of ministry. And we must remember that Jesus was anything but popular and respected by the Jewish leaders. Fitting in to the cultural expectations of His contemporaries was hardly one of His primary goals.

No, Jesus was never married, except in a spiritual sense to His bride, the church, for whom He suffered, died, and rose again, in order to bring her into an eternal relationship with Himself.[5]

Practical Results: How Both Natures Bring Benefit

The union of deity and humanity in the person of Jesus Christ is referred to in theological circles as the "hypostatic union." As dry as it may sound, this doctrine is not a dusty piece of academic trivia. It's both vibrant in expression and vital to our experience of the Christian life.

Consider the following Scripture passages, and note the benefits that believers enjoy because of the incarnation of Christ.

Mark 2:7–12

____

____

____

Hebrews 2:17

____

____

____

Hebrews 4:15

Galatians 3:20, 28–29

1 Timothy 2:5

"Thanks be to God for His indescribable gift!" the apostle Paul exclaimed (2 Corinthians 9:15). And the incarnation, deity made one with human flesh in Jesus Christ, is just that—indescribable! How can our finite minds begin to grasp such infinite mercy?

STARTING YOUR JOURNEY

If we fail to reflect on the doctrine of the incarnation, we will overlook its profound implications and application. We spent the last three lessons examining various aspects of the incarnation—the full deity and complete, sinless humanity of Jesus Christ.

We also studied several Scriptures related to this doctrine to help reinforce it. Let's try to process all of this information with an "open-book quiz."

In your own words, define the incarnation of Jesus Christ.

Where would you turn in the Bible to demonstrate the deity of Christ? List at least two passages.

Where would you turn in the Bible to show the humanity of Christ? List at least two passages.

Leader Help

The group facilitator should carefully prepare answers to these questions, using the material of lessons 7, 8, and 9. It might be fun for group members to exchange answers and critique each other, or they may simply compare answers as part of group discussion. Or the class can try to compose a single answer as a group. Be creative, but be sure to draw on previous lessons and any outside reading group members have completed.

Where would you turn in the Bible to show both the deity and humanity of Christ in one person?

In your own words, describe the importance of the doctrine of the incarnation for salvation.

Describe the importance of the incarnation for Christian living.

After you've completed these questions, return to the three charges in the "You Are Here" section of this lesson. Do you feel better equipped to handle these objections? Try responding to them again. What areas are still unclear to you?

____

____

____

____

____

The incarnation is a central doctrine that sets the Christian faith apart from false religions and even false views of Christianity. Some erred in the early church by denying the humanity of Christ (the Gnostics). Others erred by denying the deity of Christ (the Ebionites). Today, Christians can err by not understanding or being able to biblically defend the incarnation. Such a crucial doctrine ought not only demand our belief but also our attention. From this doctrine of the person of Christ, everything that follows—His suffering and death, resurrection from the dead, and ascension into heaven—has eternal significance *for us*.

He is not parted or divided into two persons, but is one and the same only-begotten Son, God, Word, Lord Jesus Christ, just as the prophets taught from the beginning about him, and as the Lord Jesus Christ himself instructed us, and as the creed of the fathers handed it down to us.[6]

—The Definition of Chalcedon, AD 451

Lesson Ten

Jesus: A Lamb Led to Slaughter

Isaiah 53:1–7; Selected Scriptures

THE HEART OF THE MATTER

Although we work hard at camouflaging its pain and denying its potency, death is a grim, harsh, ugly, and inescapable fact. We don't relish the thought of our lives ending, especially in a painful manner. What's true for us today was also true for Jesus of Nazareth—yet Jesus humbly and quietly yielded to death, allowing Himself to be led "like a lamb . . . to slaughter" (Isaiah 53:7), taking our place. Because Jesus—the God-man—died in the place of sinful humanity, His death has extraordinary significance, not only in the fields of history and theology; it has personal, eternal significance for each one of us.

Leader Help

By the end of this lesson, group members should understand that the death of Jesus Christ fulfilled God's eternal purpose of salvation, and they should be moved to examine their own response and responsibility in light of the truth that Christ died for them.

YOU ARE HERE

The Mel Gibson movie *The Passion of the Christ* stunned audiences worldwide with its shocking portrayal of the final hours of Jesus's life. In the midst of the startling, horrifying events depicted on film, one profound message united the seemingly endless barrage of brutality—*He did all of this for us*. This cinematic portrayal of the suffering and death of Christ would be just a series of bloody, violent, and pointless images without this central truth. It was predicted centuries before Jesus of Nazareth set His feet upon on this earth:

> But He was pierced through for our
> transgressions,
> He was crushed for our iniquities;
> The chastening for our well-being fell
> upon Him,
> And by His scourging we are healed.
> (Isaiah 53:5)

Leader Help

As an exercise to stimulate reflection and discussion, ask group members to bring in visual portrayals of the crucifixion—either classical or modern—by any artist in any medium (painting, sculpture, photography, and so forth). Discuss how the artist depicted Christ's suffering, the emotional response you think the artist was seeking to elicit, and the artist's apparent attitude toward Jesus's suffering and death.

If you saw the film *The Passion of the Christ*, what was your initial reaction? Describe your emotions or thoughts regarding this film or other visual representations of the same events.

One debate that arose during the release of this film concerned the question, "Who was responsible for Christ's death?" According to each of the following New Testament passages, what is the answer to that question?

John 10:17–18

Acts 2:22–23; 4:27–28

Romans 5:8

Jesus endured all of this suffering and pain willingly. He did it all for you. How does this truth affect your view of His suffering and death?

Max Lucado, in his book *No Wonder They Call Him the Savior*, writes of the grandeur of God's dramatic display of love on the cross. His words serve as a reminder that although the death of Christ was gruesome, bloody, and disturbing, it marks the center of God's plan of salvation and the purpose of the incarnation of the God-man. He writes:

> Nearing the climax of the story, God, motivated by love and directed by divinity, surprised everyone. He became a man. . . .
>
> But as beautiful as this act of incarnation was, it was not the zenith. Like a master painter God reserved his masterpiece until the end. All the earlier acts of love had been leading to this one. The angels hushed and the heavens paused to witness the finale. God unveils the canvas and the ultimate act of creative compassion is revealed.
>
> God on a cross.[1]

DISCOVERING THE WAY

"Born to die." This phrase has been applied to many hardened criminals. But the cruel shoe fits the sinless Christ better than it has for any person in history's hall of shame. What many onlookers believed to be the senseless suffering of an innocent man was, in reality, the cornerstone of God's plan of salvation and victory over sin and death.

Death: Jesus's Constant Companion

The destiny of Christ had been determined in eternity before the foundations of the world. The prophetic obituary of Isaiah 53 perched like a vulture over the manger of Christ. Sorrow, grief, and pain stood idly by, carefully watching and waiting for their time to come. Every day, the shadow of the cross stretched long across Christ's path. Before He reached the age of two, an assassination plot by King Herod attempted to end His tender life (Matthew 2:16). By the time He was a young boy, He had memorized the Old Testament prophecies of His death. At thirty-three, when most men are still getting their careers off the ground, His life was about to end.

Read Isaiah 53:1–3, a prophecy written about seven centuries before Christ's birth. According to these verses, how were people expected to respond to the Messiah?

As you read Isaiah 53:4–7, note each of the things the Messiah was predicted to do.

Our teacher of these things is Jesus Christ, who also was born for this purpose, and was crucified under Pontius Pilate, procurator of Judaea, in the times of Tiberius Caesar; and . . . we reasonably worship Him, having learned that He is the Son of the true God Himself.[2]

—Justin Martyr
(c. AD 155)

Not only was the death of Christ prophesied in the Old Testament, He foretold it Himself. His predictions are recorded in several New Testament passages.

Read the following passages regarding Christ's own predictions of His suffering and death, then use one word to describe the various responses of His listeners.

Matthew 16:21–23

____

____

____

Matthew 17:22–23

____

____

____

Matthew 20:17–21

____

____

____

Matthew 26:1–13

____

____

____

John 13:21

Why do you think His listeners responded in these ways?

Try to put yourself in the disciples' shoes. How would you respond if the person you were convinced was God's agent of righteousness and judgment said He had to suffer and die?

In the dark of night, Christ celebrated the Last Supper with His disciples. Jesus was about to be betrayed and denied by those who had been closest to Him (John 13:21–38). No wonder they were deeply troubled! And it came as no surprise to them that their Savior, who had once calmed both wind and waves, would now speak to calm their troubled hearts.

Read John 14:1–3 and 16:7–8, 13. If Jesus had *not* endured His prophesied suffering and death, what promises from these passages would remain unfulfilled?

After the Last Supper, Jesus and His disciples sang a hymn and departed to the Mount of Olives (Matthew 26:30). And there, His trials and suffering began.

Arrest and Trials: The Shadow Lengthens

Though Jesus warned that all of His disciples would fall away in the midst of His greatest hour of suffering, they refused to believe Him (Matthew 26:31–35). Little did they know that, contrary to their most fervent vows and bold claims, they would all be guilty of the confession in Isaiah 53:6: "All of us like sheep have gone astray, each of us has turned to his own way."

Nevertheless, Jesus led the disciples to the small, intimate garden spot known as Gethsemane to pray (Matthew 26:36). He asked the others to wait while He took Peter, James, and John deeper into the garden. In those moments, Christ stood on a precipice overlooking the valley of death. For the world to have light and life, He would have to surrender to the darkness of death. Fear and dread knotted His stomach. Such unbearable agony gripped Him that He began to sweat drops of blood as He prayed for His Father to remove the cup of suffering from Him (Luke 22:42–44). Yet even in His anguished prayer, He yielded Himself to the ultimate will of the Father.

Read Matthew 26:38–39. How are both Jesus's deity and humanity evident in His prayer to the Father? Give specific examples.

Leader Text

If possible, divide your large group into several smaller groups or pairs, and assign each group one of the passages beginning on this page. Allow the groups a few minutes to answer the question in regard to their particular passage. Each group should then share one practical application or personal response to their passage.

According to the following passages from Hebrews, what does the suffering of the God-man mean for us personally?

Hebrews 2:17–18

Hebrews 4:14–16

Hebrews 5:7–9

Hebrews 7:26–27

Hebrews 9:11–14

____

____

____

Hebrews 9:26–28

____

____

____

Though Jesus's last night on earth was long and torturous, the events happened in rapid-fire succession. The vigilante mob arrived. Judas's kiss sealed the betrayal. The Shepherd was taken captive, and His sheep were scattered (Matthew 26:47–56). Six unjust trials convened that sleepless night. The first three were conducted by the Jewish authorities and dealt with religious questions (John 18:12–24; Matthew 26:57–68; 27:1). The final three involved civil questions and were conducted by the Roman authorities (Matthew 27:2–14; Luke 23:5–25). Because the Sanhedrin could not legally carry out an execution without the permission of Rome, they turned Christ over to the pagan authorities, and by lies, manipulation, and political maneuvering they secured the God-man's death sentence (Matthew 27:24–26).

The Trials of Jesus Christ

Trial	Officiating Authority	Scripture	Accusation	Legality	Type	Result
1	Annas, ex-high priest of the Jews (AD 6–15)	John 18:13–23	Trumped-up charges of irreverence to Annas	ILLEGAL! Held at night, no specific charges, prejudice, violence	Jewish and Religious	Found guilty of irreverence and rushed to Caiaphas
2	Caiaphas—Annas's son-in-law—and the Sanhedrin (AD 18–36)	Matthew 26:57–68 Mark 14:53–65 John 18:24	Claiming to be the Messiah, the Son of God—blasphemy (worthy of death under Jewish law)	ILLEGAL! Held at night, false witnesses, prejudice, violence	Jewish and Religious	Declared guilty of blasphemy and rushed to the Sanhedrin (Jewish supreme court)
3	The Sanhedrin—seventy ruling men of Israel (their word was needed before He could be taken to Roman officials)	Mark 15:1 Luke 22:66–71	Claiming to be the Son of God—blasphemy	ILLEGAL! Accusation switched, no witnesses, improper voting	Jewish and Religious	Declared guilty of blasphemy and rushed to Roman official, Pilate
4	Pilate, governor of Judea, who was already in "hot water" with Rome (AD 26–36)	Matthew 27:11–14 Mark 15:1–5 Luke 23:1–7 John 18:28–38	Treason (accusation was changed, since treason was worthy of capital punishment in Rome)	ILLEGAL! Christ was kept under arrest, although He was found innocent. No defense attorney, violence	Roman and Civil	Found innocent . . . but rushed to Herod Antipas; mob overruled Pilate
5	Herod Antipas, governor of Galilee (4 BC–AD 39)	Luke 23:8–12	No accusation was made	ILLEGAL! No grounds, mockery in courtroom, no defense attorney, violence	Roman and Civil	Mistreated and mocked; returned to Pilate without decision made by Herod
6	Pilate (second time)	Matthew 27:15–26 Mark 15:6–15 Luke 23:18–25 John 18:39–19:16	Treason, though not proven (Pilate bargained with the mob, putting Christ on a level with Barabbas, a criminal)	ILLEGAL! Without proof of guilt, Pilate allowed an innocent man to be condemned.	Roman and Civil	Found innocent, but Pilate "washed his hands" and allowed Him to be crucified

DIGGING DEEPER
The Meaning of Christ's Atonement

What exactly does it mean that Christ's death was "atonement" for our sins? What benefits do believers receive because of His finished work on the cross? Some theologians limit the benefit of Christ's death either to a moral influence ("He gave up His life for those He loves, so we should do the same") or even to a social statement ("He was assassinated by the elite, patriarchal establishment because He took a stand for the poor and marginal members of society"). These ideas limit the person of Jesus to His humanity and render His death merely a natural rather than a supernatural event.

However, because Jesus is the incarnate God-man, His death was far more than just a moral example or social statement. He was the once-for-all *sacrifice* for sin (Ephesians 5:2; Hebrews 10:11–14). His death was also a *substitution* for all mankind, as Christ died *in place of* sinners (2 Corinthians 5:14–15; 1 Peter 3:18). He provided a payment for sin, a *ransom* to buy back or *redeem* believers from sin and death (Matthew 20:28; Romans 6:23; 1 Timothy 2:6). His death was also an *expiation*, "the removal of the guilt of sin,"[3] effecting *forgiveness* for believers by His blood (Matthew 26:28; Ephesians 1:7–8). At the same time, His death satisfied God's wrath—providing *propitiation* (Romans 3:24–26; 1 John 2:2)—bringing about our *reconciliation*

Continued on next page

Continued from previous page

or mending of our broken relationship with the holy God (Romans 5:10; 2 Corinthians 5:18; Colossians 1:19–22). In all of these, Jesus Christ—through the weakest, most humiliating event of His life—became the victor, conquering death and destroying the powers of sin and Satan (1 Corinthians 15:55; Hebrews 2:14; 1 John 3:8).[4]

The Cross: *Tetelestai*

A sleepless night of indignity . . . the slander of false witnesses . . . cruel beatings . . . a crown of thorns digging into His brow . . . a robe and scepter of mock royalty . . . more bloody scourging . . . more angry mocking. By nine o'clock in the morning, Jesus's hands and feet were nailed to a rough-cut cross that was then dropped with a dull thud into a hole in Golgotha's peak. From noon until three o'clock that afternoon, darkness fell over the earth—truly the darkest hours in human history.

In the last moments of His earthly life, Jesus cried out loud enough for all to hear, "*Tetelestai!*"—"It is finished!" The crucifixion was the darkest moment in history, but these words pierced through the blackness like a radiant beam of sunlight.

These words don't refer simply to the completion of Christ's suffering, but to the completion of the monumental task He was born to do—willingly relinquishing His own life in order to "save His people from their sins" (Matthew 1:21). The timbers of the cross formed the bridge spanning hell's chasm, uniting earth and heaven, bridging the gap sin had created between God and man. With the words "It is finished!" the bridge was complete. Jesus's cry was one of victory, one of accomplishment—with these words, chains fell away, prison walls crumbled, barriers were destroyed, and gates that had been closed for thousands of years began to turn on their rusty hinges.

And yes, His cry was also one of relief. Jesus could now exchange His thorns for a crown, His nakedness for a robe, His disgrace for glory, His wounds for worship, and His loneliness for heavenly fellowship with His Father.

STARTING YOUR JOURNEY

The death of Christ represented more than just the inspiring martyrdom of a godly man. His death was the ultimate sacrifice of the God-man—effecting our salvation. His once-for-all payment of the price for sin demands a response from each and every person on earth.

If you do not have a personal relationship with Jesus Christ, it's as if you are treading water in a sea of guilt. Life may appear calm, and you may even feel that you have everything under control. But one day, you'll sink. The only life preserver is Jesus; the only way to heaven is by walking across the bridge of the cross.

Since the Lord thus has redeemed us through His own blood, giving His soul for our souls, and His flesh for our flesh, and has also poured out the Spirit of the Father for the union and communion of God and man, imparting indeed God to men by means of the Spirit, and, on the other hand, attaching man to God by His own incarnation, and bestowing upon us at His coming immortality durably and truly, by means of communion with God,—all the doctrines of the heretics fall to ruin.[5]

—Irenaeus of Lyons (c. AD 185)

If you're sinking in sin or if you're not sure how Christ's payment for sin applies to you personally, read the "How to Begin a Relationship with God" section at the end of this workbook. When you finish, note your thoughts or response here:

____

____

____

____

____

If you've already made the decision to accept Christ's payment for your sin, write down your reflections on how He has changed your life—and thank Jesus for spanning the chasm between death and life *for you*.

____

____

____

____

____

Sharing the good news that Christ died for us in order to pay the price for our sins and provide those who believe in Him with eternal life has become more and more difficult in an increasingly pagan and anti-Christian society. However, in the early church Christians often referred to the prophecies of the suffering, death, and resurrection of the Messiah to convince unbelievers of the truth of Christianity. Those same prophecies can be used today to confront skeptics with the way of truth. The following study questions—which may take some additional time to complete—should help strengthen your own understanding and confidence in Christ's work and also equip you to share the good news with others.

Read Isaiah 53:1–12 and Psalm 22:1–24. Note the words in these passages that refer to Christ's suffering for us, His death, and His ultimate resurrection.

	Isaiah 53:1–12	Psalm 22:1–24
Suffering		
Death		
Resurrection		

Read Acts 8:26–35. How could you use these prophecies about the suffering, death, and resurrection of the Messiah to help convince those who don't believe that Jesus was more than a mere human figure who lived and died?

Based on this prophetic evidence, write a paragraph or so addressing an unbeliever who claims that the Bible is just a human work or that Jesus's death was just a human death. For additional insight into the prophecies concerning Christ, consult section 3 of "Resources for Probing Further," page 240.

In this lesson, we focused on the death of Christ as the fulfillment of the purpose and plan of God. Through Old Testament prophecies and the words of Jesus Himself, we have come to understand that His crucifixion has supreme significance. The suffering He endured wasn't pointless; He purchased eternal salvation for all who believe. Have you been moved to examine your own response to this good news? Have you taken the crucial first step on the way of truth? Are you leading others to the same path?

Lesson Eleven

Jesus: Triumphant over the Grave

John 19:30–20:29

THE HEART OF THE MATTER

Christ's triumph over the grave is the unique, distinctive trait of Christianity. It designates Christianity, the faith based on Jesus's person and work, the *only* true faith and renders all other versions of history, religion, and theology as dead as death itself. But the truth of Christ's resurrection affects more than history and theology. Because He lives, we can face each day with confident faith in the one true God—the only one who has the power to overcome the grave!

YOU ARE HERE

That morning dawned like any other in the ancient Roman city of Pompeii. Children played just as they had the day before and for months and years before that. Men and women went about their business as usual: working hard in the bright sunlight and then resting in the cool shade of the mountain; worshiping their idols in the pagan temples; eating, drinking, and living their normal lives. Yet in a few precious hours,

Leader Help

By the end of this lesson, group members should be confident in the truth of Christ's bodily resurrection and feel equipped to counter arguments that would seek to challenge this truth.

they would be no more; the fury of Mount Vesuvius would erupt to encase Pompeii and its people in a tomb of lava for centuries to come.

About forty years before the destruction of Pompeii, another eruption took place that not only shook the foundations of earth; it shook the foundations of heaven as well. An ordinary woman had come to visit the tomb of her beloved Friend. But instead of finding the tranquility of a garden tomb, she discovered an open grave—the body missing, the stone rolled away. She fled in terror and grief, not understanding that the tomb had erupted with the power of God. The crucified Son of God had risen, triumphantly conquering death and bringing new life to a human race entombed in sin.

Leader Help

At least one or two elements of each of the following questions should be addressed as a group to help each group member recognize the obvious contrast between a world redeemed by Christ's resurrection and a world without redemption.

Read 1 Corinthians 15:14–19. If Jesus of Nazareth had not truly risen from the dead, what would you have to say . . .

. . . about Jesus?

. . . about the New Testament?

. . . about the Christian faith?

. . . about your salvation?

On the other hand, because Jesus really *did* rise from the dead (1 Corinthians 15:20–27), how do you view . . .

. . . Jesus?

. . . the Bible?

. . . Christianity?

. . . God?

. . . the world?

Clearly the resurrection of Christ holds the Christian faith and history together like a lynchpin. If Jesus did not rise from the dead, Christianity would be no more authoritative than the pagan religions of Pompeii. On the other hand, if He really did triumph over the grave, this event gives Christianity a unique distinctive: its Founder lives! All other religions and all other "gods" are rendered false. Everything must now be understood in light of the resurrection. In short, Jesus Christ rose from the dead, and this event serves as a singular signpost pointing to the only way of truth in a world of fiction.

DOORWAY TO HISTORY
The Resurrection and Other Religions

Most nonbiblical religions, philosophies, and movements share at least one thing in common: they originated with a compelling individual—a person so fascinating to his followers that something of his personality continues to hold sway to this day. But one profound difference distinguishes Christianity and its Founder, Jesus of Nazareth.

Religion or Philosophy	Founder	Approximate Date of Death	Founder's Status
Taoism	Lao-tzu	550 BC	Dead
Buddhism	Gautama Buddha	483 BC	Dead
Platonism	Plato	348 BC	Dead
Christianity	Jesus	AD 30	**ALIVE**
Gnosticism	Valentinus	AD 160	Dead
Islam	Muhammad	AD 632	Dead
Mormonism	Joseph Smith	AD 1844	Dead
Evolutionism	Charles Darwin	AD 1882	Dead
Scientology	L. Ron Hubbard	AD 1986	Dead

While all other religious leaders and philosophers remain dead and buried, Jesus Christ is alive! The bodily resurrection sets Christianity apart as the only religion that claims its founder lives . . . and even offers historical evidence to support that bold claim!

DISCOVERING THE WAY

In 1 Corinthians 1:22, Paul wrote, "Jews ask for signs and Greeks search for wisdom." Today's skeptics are no different—they demand rational proof or showy, phenomenal miracles to demonstrate the truthfulness of the Christian faith beyond doubt.

According to Matthew 12:38–40, the resurrection was the great sign that authenticated Jesus's person and work. Instead of displaying nickel-and-dime shows of power, Jesus offered a sign so spectacular that one would have had to be blind to miss it. The sad truth is, many who lived in Christ's day were spiritually blind. Today, many scholars are also blind to the reality of the resurrection, sometimes refusing to examine the historical evidences because of their presuppositions against the possibility of miraculous events in history. However, the historical evidence for the resurrection is clear for those who have eyes to see and ears to hear (Matthew 13:14–16; Acts 28:23–28).

Why do people deny the resurrection today? What reasons do they give? What sort of objections have you heard?

Do you feel equipped to counter these objections to the resurrection, especially if they challenge the truthfulness or reliability of the Gospel accounts? If so, how would you counter them? What proof would you offer?

____

____

____

____

____

Pertinent Issues Related to Jesus's Resurrection

In the past—though not as often today—skeptics have sometimes sought to explain away the evidence of Christ's resurrection by suggesting that Jesus didn't really die. In fact, one of the earliest Gnostic heretics, Basilides, taught that Jesus tricked His attackers into crucifying the wrong man! Irenaeus, an early church father, describes Basilides's strange opinion:

> Wherefore he did not himself suffer death, but Simon, a certain man of Cyrene, being compelled, bore the cross in his stead; so that this latter being transfigured by him, that he might be thought to be Jesus, was crucified, through ignorance and error, while Jesus himself received the form of Simon, and, standing by, laughed at them.[1]

In the nineteenth and twentieth centuries, denials of the resurrection became a bit more sophisticated but remained very strange in nature. Some said Jesus merely fainted from the trauma of the cross and later revived in the coolness of the tomb. The controversial film *The Last Temptation of Christ* portrayed Jesus as coming down from the cross, living the life of a normal man, getting married, and starting a family. In the face of ancient heresies that denied the true death of Christ, the eyewitnesses of the death and resurrection recorded the true, literal death of Jesus in a clear, deliberate manner. The gospel of John was written by an eyewitness of the events (John 19:35; 21:24; 1 John 1:1–3). John provides an excellent perspective on the reality of the death and resurrection of Christ.

As you read John 19:30–42, note the evidence that Jesus really died rather than merely appeared to die.

____

____

____

____

____

Why was it important for John to demonstrate that Jesus really died?

Not only did John want to reinforce the fact of Christ's real suffering and death, he also wanted to reassure his readers that Jesus rose from the dead. To that end, he provided a record of circumstantial material evidence, and he also described Christ's numerous appearances to various groups of people after the resurrection.

What material evidence for Jesus's resurrection, both physical and circumstantial, is recorded in John 20:1–10? List as many different answers as possible.

Leader Help
Depending on time constraints and the personality of your group, the following question might be fun to answer by dividing group members into teams and competing to see who can come up with the most observable evidence for a bodily resurrection.

Having therefore received their orders and being fully assured by the resurrection of our Lord Jesus Christ and full of faith in the Word of God, they went forth with the firm assurance that the Holy Spirit gives, preaching the good news that the kingdom of God was about to come.[2]

—Clement of Rome (c. AD 95)

What did the disciples conclude regarding this evidence?

One of the earliest arguments against the bodily resurrection leveled by Christ's opponents accused the disciples of stealing the body and then claiming that Jesus rose from the dead (Matthew 28:13–15). Since then, others have suggested the same thing—that *someone* stole the body. But logically, who would have taken it? Neither the Jews nor the Romans would have stolen it, because the last thing they wanted was an empty tomb. They wanted proof that Christ was dead and buried. If either group had stolen the body, they would merely have had to produce it, and they would have discredited the disciples' claim of the resurrection. But they were never able to do so!

The Roman guards, whose very lives were at stake as they guarded the body, wouldn't have dared to steal it or allow it to be stolen. The alarm and even disbelief expressed by the disciples precludes them from being suspects, and a conspiracy by the disciples falls apart when we realize that most of the original followers of Jesus were killed for their faith in the risen Lord! In short, neither friend nor foe had a logical motive—or desire—to take Jesus's body. All the evidence points to Christ's literal, bodily resurrection.

Besides circumstantial evidence, John and other apostles recorded no fewer than eleven physical encounters with the risen Christ that occurred at different times, in different places, and with different individuals and groups. These were not merely misty, surreal "visions." The disciples spoke with Jesus, touched Him, and even sat down and ate meals with Him.

Read the following passages, and identify the individuals or groups (by name, if possible) who witnessed the resurrected Jesus. Give a brief description of each reaction to Jesus's appearance.

Luke 24:13–35	
John 20:18–20	
John 20:26–28	
John 21:2–4	
Acts 1:1–4, 12–15, 21–23	
1 Corinthians 15:3–8	

For I know and believe that he was in the flesh even after the resurrection; and when he came to Peter and those with him, he said to them: "Take hold of me; handle me and see that I am not a disembodied demon." And immediately they touched him and believed.[3]

—Ignatius of Antioch (c. AD 110)

Some skeptics have argued that all of these people merely had grief-induced hallucinations. However, Paul said Jesus once appeared to more than five hundred people at one time (1 Corinthians 15:6), and he even pointed out that most of those people were still alive at the time of his writing, able to testify! For so many people to have shared the same "hallucination" at the same time strains the imagination far more than the probability of Christ's bodily resurrection.

Historical Results of the Resurrection

The resurrection of Christ was accompanied not only by a great deal of circumstantial material evidence and many eyewitness encounters but also by historical results. We read in the last chapter that at the time of the crucifixion, the disciples scattered like scared sheep (Matthew 26:56). Then, after seeing the empty tomb, they concluded that someone had stolen the body, and they went to their own homes in mourning (John 20:2, 8–10). There they stayed, cowering and grief-stricken, hidden away in fear of the Jews (John 20:19). Had Jesus been truly dead and gone, they would have eventually fled to continue their lives in another place, never to be "duped" by a false messiah again. But He had risen—He was and is alive!

After they saw the risen Christ, this weak-kneed band of deserters turned the world upside down with their passionate preaching (Acts 17:6)! Even Peter, who had denied Christ so emphatically, preached boldly about Him in the very city where Jesus had been recently executed (Acts 2:14–36). The descent of the Holy Spirit and the birth of the church are other historical ramifications of Christ's resurrection (Acts 1–2). In fact, if Jesus had not truly risen from the dead, the transformation of His disciples, the birth of the church, its astounding expansion, and the selfless martyrdoms of the apostles would be unexplainable. Why? Because if that were true, the disciples, who knew Jesus best, would have lived and died for a fictional account, a lie they had created.

Paul acknowledged this truth:

> If Christ has not been raised, then our preaching is vain, your faith also is vain. Moreover we are even found to be false witnesses of God, because we testified against God that He raised Christ, whom He did not raise, if in fact the dead are not raised. (1 Corinthians 15:14–15)

But Paul's faith was not in vain, and his testimony was not false. Clement, the pastor of Rome at the end of the first century—and perhaps the one-time companion of Paul (Philippians 4:3)—reflected on the stand Paul took for the truth of the resurrection:

> After he had been seven times in chains, had been driven into exile, had been stoned, and had preached in the East and in the West, he won the genuine glory for his faith, having taught righteousness to the whole world and having reached the farthest limits of the West. Finally, when he had given his testimony before the rulers, he thus departed from the world and went to the holy place, having become an outstanding example of patient endurance.[4]

No modern writer of fiction or contemporary critic of the resurrection could ever boast such a seal of authenticity marking the truthfulness of his or her claims.

STARTING YOUR JOURNEY

Paul said, "If Christ has not been raised, your faith is worthless" (1 Corinthians 15:17). The resurrection is the keystone of the Christian faith. While we've seen that the incarnation forms the gravitational center of theology and the sacrificial death of Christ marks the culmination of His earthly mission, both of these claims are nullified if Jesus of Nazareth did not rise from the dead. The resurrection is the sign that points us to Jesus as the God-man who died for us. It is the seal of authentication upon our faith and the promise of our future resurrection and our eternal life.

In "Resources for Probing Further," section 8, "Works on the Resurrection of Jesus Christ," you'll find resources to help strengthen your confidence in the resurrection of Jesus and equip you to counter those who reject this essential truth. After reviewing a selection or two from this list, what would you categorize as the three greatest objections to the resurrection? (NOTE: If you cannot find these recommended resources, you might be able to research this question from your own library or even through Internet resources.)

How would you answer these objections? Be specific.

Leader Help

The following questions will be most effective if your group works together to identify several objections to the resurrection. Then, break your group into teams, and assign each smaller group to study one specific objection using books from "Resources for Probing Further," section 8, on page 243. When you meet together next, set aside a few minutes at the beginning of the session to allow each team to share their answers with the whole group.

Never were the arms of God opened so wide as when they were outstretched on the cross. Like a father embracing his prodigal son, the arms of Jesus reached out to give the embrace of forgiveness to all who would come to Him. We pray that God will give you the grace to look at the nail prints in the hands of the risen Savior and fall on your face before Him, as Thomas did, proclaiming: "My Lord and my God!" The resurrection assures us not only that Jesus is God, but that we are forgiven and also will be raised to eternal life (1 Corinthians 15). Be confident in the truth!

Lesson Twelve

Jesus: Ascended and Seated in Heaven

Acts 1:6–11; Ephesians 1:18–23

THE HEART OF THE MATTER

Without question, the most neglected area of study regarding the Lord Jesus Christ is that of His present ministry. Like the disciples, we might be tempted to jump straight from His resurrection to His glorious return. But consider the truth that Jesus rose from the dead and ascended into heaven. What does this mean for history . . . for theology . . . for ministry? These questions are not simply theoretical in nature. They impact powerfully our view of the church, the world, and our own lives.

Leader Help

By the end of this lesson, group members should be able to describe the present work of Christ at the right hand of the Father and express practical applications for their own ministry involvement.

YOU ARE HERE

Naysayers often ridiculed the doctrine of Christ's ascension as a convenient excuse to cover up the mysterious absence of Jesus's physical body. Of course, such critics have also rejected the resurrection of Christ as a Christian "myth," so it follows that they must reject everything believers assert about Jesus beyond that crucial event. Yet the doctrine of the ascension can also cause believers to scratch their heads and ponder many nagging questions. And very few seek to fully understand the truth, though it holds much personal, practical meaning for our spiritual lives.

Leader Help
Encourage group members to answer these questions quickly and without consulting each other or their Bibles. Their first impressions will contribute most effectively to the goal of this exercise.

Why do you think Jesus would have chosen to leave His disciples after His resurrection?

What do you think the world would have been like if Jesus had simply stayed on earth? What do you think He would have done here?

Understanding that Jesus ascended into heaven, why do you think He has remained there for so long?

How did the disciples benefit from Christ's ascension?

How did the world benefit?

How did you benefit?

DISCOVERING THE WAY

Why did Jesus leave? What is He doing now? When He ascended, did His position in relation to God and in regard to His heavenly responsibilities change from what it was before He became a man? What does the ascension mean for us? Let's take a closer look at the reality of the ascension and enthronement of Christ and especially consider its significance in our own lives.

The Ascension: When Jesus Christ Left Earth

Acts 1:1–11 informs us that Jesus remained in contact with His followers for forty days after His resurrection (compare with Luke 24:13–49). Then it was time for Him to depart and return to His rightful place in heaven. Moments before He ascended, the disciples eagerly raised their hands to pose a question to their teacher.

Read Acts 1:6. What burning question consumed the disciples' minds?

____

____

____

According to Matthew 19:28, what future role would the disciples play in Christ's glorious kingdom?

Read Jesus's answer to their question in Acts 1:7–8. What should the disciples have focused on?

Compare the tasks given to the disciples upon Jesus's departure to heaven in these two passages. What were they to do? How were they equipped to accomplish it?

Leader Help
Depending on your time constraints, you might choose to write this chart on a board and work through it as a group, or those group members who prepared ahead could share their findings with everyone else.

	Matthew 28:18–20	Acts 1:8
What were the disciples to do?		
How were they equipped to do it?		

Following His promise regarding the Holy Spirit's presence and power, Jesus spoke His last words on earth and ascended into heaven (Acts 1:9). As He rose gradually into the clouds and disappeared, the awestruck disciples craned their necks and squinted into the sky, seeking one last look at their Savior.

Admittedly, at first glance the doctrine of the ascension seems like the clouds into which Christ ascended—distant and nebulous. However, understanding the ascension contributes practically to our faith and spiritual lives in at least four ways. First, it helps us appreciate the credibility of Christ. Jesus said He would have to leave the disciples one day (John 13:33, 36; 14:1–6); and because they actually, physically saw Him leave, their experience underscored the credibility of Christ's teaching. Second, if Christ had not ascended into heaven, the Holy Spirit could not have been given to us (John 16:7). Third, without His ascension, we would never have received our spiritual gifts (Ephesians 4:7–8). Fourth, in Jesus's literal, bodily ascension, we are reminded that His return will also be a literal, bodily return (Acts 1:11).

Consider the following Scripture passages. If Christ had not ascended to the Father, what promises would never have been fulfilled? Specifically, what would believers never have received?

John 16:7–11

Ephesians 4:8–16

How do these promises equip you to fulfill the Great Commission—the work of passing on the Christian faith to others (Matthew 28:19–20)?

It was prophesied that, after the ascent of Christ to heaven, He would deliver us from error and give us gifts. The words are these: "He ascended up on high; He led captivity captive; He gave gifts to men."[1]

—Justin Martyr
(c. AD 165)

Entrance: When Jesus Christ Returned to Heaven

Moving from Acts 1 to Ephesians 1, we leave earth and glimpse the heavenly side of the ascension. In direct contrast to the acts of Jesus's torturers, who gave Him a crown of thorns, scepter, and robe in blatant mockery, the Father's act of receiving His Son into heaven demonstrated His approval of Christ and His redemptive mission. The Father, in a royal coronation ceremony, placed the King of Kings on His rightful throne. In subjecting all things under Christ, the Father gave Him dominion not only over His enemies but over the church as well (Ephesians 1:18–23).

Based on the following Scriptures, briefly summarize what Christ's ascension meant for . . .

. . . the nations (Psalm 110:1–2; Revelation 1:5).

____

____

____

. . . the church (Colossians 1:16–18; Ephesians 1:22–23).

____

____

____

. . . the whole universe (Ephesians 1:18–21; Philippians 2:9–11).

TRUTH OR FICTION?
Did a Unified Church Develop from Diversity and Conflict?

Some modern historians and theologians propose that the early church was characterized by "radical diversity." They argue that we cannot legitimately speak of a unified "Christianity" during that time, but rather, that the early church consisted of competing "Christianities."[2] Having denied the reality of the resurrection, these scholars are faced with explaining how Christianity developed a unified confession of faith and a standard body (canon) of sacred Scriptures. These historians believe that the "orthodox" church was the end result of many decades of conflict, and they also believe that the Catholic church even forged documents like Acts and 2 Peter in order to paint a false picture of unity and harmony in the early church. Today, works of fiction like *The Da Vinci Code* and groups like the Jesus Seminar presuppose this view of the early church.

Continued on next page

Continued from previous page

However, if Jesus truly rose from the dead, ascended into heaven, and sent the Holy Spirit just as the earliest eyewitnesses claimed, then the "diversity and conflict" version of early church history could not be correct. The continuing headship of Christ over the worldwide church (Colossians 1:18) and the abiding presence of Christ through the indwelling Spirit (John 14:16–18) both guarantee that the true church would remain united around the central doctrines of the Christian faith, even in the face of internal and external conflict. Irenaeus—a student of John's disciple, Polycarp—described the unity of the church near the end of the second century in terms that still reflect the church today:

> The Church, though dispersed throughout the whole world, even to the ends of the earth, has received from the apostles and their disciples this faith: [She believes] in one God, the Father Almighty, Maker of heaven, and earth, and the sea, and all things that are in them; and in one Christ Jesus, the Son of God, who became incarnate for our salvation; and in the Holy Spirit, who proclaimed through the prophets the dispensations of God, and the advents, and the birth from a virgin, and the passion, and the resurrection from the dead, and the ascension into heaven in the flesh of

> the beloved Christ Jesus, our Lord, and His [future] manifestation from heaven in the glory of the Father . . .
>
> As I have already observed, the Church, having received this preaching and this faith, although scattered throughout the whole world, yet, as if occupying but one house, carefully preserves it. . . . For, although the languages of the world are dissimilar, yet the import of the tradition is one and the same.[3]

Modern, liberal scholars attempt to revise the history of the church to reflect their own social and theological agendas. However, believers in the biblical Christian faith summarized in the early confessions can be confident that theirs is the true faith "once for all handed down to the saints" (Jude 3).[4] The presence of Christ through the Holy Spirit is our assurance that even if the church strays into conflict and error, God will preserve and renew it for His glory (Matthew 16:18; 28:20; John 16:13).

Seated: When Jesus Was Enthroned

Although Christ completed His earthly mission of redemption (Hebrews 10:12), His heavenly ministry and involvement with us as the Head of the church continues. Jesus presently functions in three primary ways in our lives: as our High Priest and Mediator; as our Lord and Master; and as our Companion and

Friend. These specific benefits of Christ's ascension and enthronement encourage and equip us to carry out the work for which He has commissioned us.

First, because of His ascension, *Jesus Christ is now our High Priest and Mediator*. Jesus, the God-man, is an advocate for us with the Father (1 Timothy 2:5; 1 John 2:1). Because His priesthood is permanent, Christ will always stand before God, defend us against Satan's accusations, and constantly intercede to preserve our salvation, forgive our sin, and relieve our guilt (Romans 8:33–39).

Read Romans 8:33–39. How should the amazing benefits of Christ's intercession encourage you to be personally involved in sharing the Christian faith with your family and friends? If Christ were not making intercession in these ways, what might thwart your involvement in the Great Commission of Matthew 28:19–20?

Second, because of His ascension, *Jesus Christ is now our sovereign Lord and Master*. Jesus is involved intimately with humankind. He sovereignly calls out a people for Himself, sovereignly functions as the head of the church, and sovereignly directs our lives.

Read Hebrews 2:7–8. How should the truth of Christ's sovereign lordship over our lives—and over the lives of even the most hardened non-Christians—affect our attitudes and actions as we contend for the faith and seek to make disciples?

____

____

____

____

____

If Christ were not exercising His lordship, how do you think your attempts at spreading the gospel would be more difficult? Be specific.

____

____

____

____

____

Third, because of His ascension, *Jesus Christ is now our constant Companion and Friend.* The writer to the Hebrews underscored repeatedly the deity and majesty of the enthroned Savior, yet he also emphasized carefully that the sovereign Lord is a close companion (Hebrews 2:11; 6:17–18). A true friend isn't capricious, on-again/off-again, or fickle.

Having been carried up to heaven, [He] sitteth on the right hand of the Father, and has been glorified by Him as the Resurrection of the dead. Moreover, He is the Salvation of the lost, the Light to those dwelling in darkness, the Redemption to those who have been born; the Shepherd of the saved, and the Bridegroom of the Church; the Charioteer of the cherubim, the Leader of the angelic host; God of God; Jesus Christ our Saviour.[5]

—Irenaeus of Lyons
(c. AD 185)

A real friend is someone you can count on in times of sorrow as well as in times of joy.

Read John 15:15–16. How should the truth of Christ's intimate fellowship with us motivate you to bear fruit for Him in your life?

How does your attitude toward evangelism change when you view it as an invitation into a heartfelt, personal relationship rather than simply convincing a person of rational facts?

The Ascension: An Ending	*The Ascension: A Beginning*
The disciples no longer see Jesus on earth.	The disciples must walk by faith and dependence on the Holy Spirit and the revelation of Scripture.
The disciples no longer feel the physical comfort of His presence.	Jesus ministers to the disciples in new ways: He will intercede on their behalf before God (Romans 8:34) and send the Holy Spirit to empower them (Acts 1:8).
Christ's mission to atone for the sins of the world is finished.	Christ's ministry as the advocate for believers against Satan's accusations is just beginning (1 John 2:1).
Christ's descent into the depths of human limitations and suffering is over.	In His glorified body, Christ enjoys an exalted relationship over creation at the right hand of God that will never end.

We observed that Christ ascended and sent the Holy Spirit in order to bring salvation to the ends of the earth, but why has He been gone for so long? Why hasn't He returned yet? After reading the following Scriptures, how would you answer somebody who asked you that question?

Romans 2:4 2 Peter 3:3–9 Revelation 2:21

____

____

____

____

____

The disciples eagerly expected the coming kingdom to arrive prior to Christ's ascension (Acts 1:6). However, they soon discovered that the return of Christ in judgment and glory would come unexpectedly at a later time (1 Thessalonians 5:1–2; 2 Peter 3:10).

According to the following passages, what should the attitude and actions of believers be in light of Jesus's imminent return?

Romans 13:11–14

____

____

1 Corinthians 11:23–26

____

____

Hebrews 10:23

____

____

2 Timothy 4:7–8

____

____

Titus 2:11–14

____

____

James 5:7–9

____

____

1 John 3:2–3

____

____

STARTING YOUR JOURNEY

The ascension of Christ marked the end of His earthly ministry and the beginning of the church's earthly mission. The Lord's enthronement as our Mediator, Master, and Friend marked the beginning of the Holy Spirit's ministry of convicting unbelievers and gifting, equipping, and empowering the saints. Therefore, the ascension of Christ is really about our unchanging mission in a changing world—it is vitally important in Christian doctrine and full of practical value for our spiritual lives.

Thus far, the lessons in this workbook have been designed to enlighten your mind to the problem of false teaching, bolster your confidence in Scripture, and equip you to take a stand for the truth of Jesus Christ. But if these lessons only accomplish those goals and do not result in encouraging your active involvement in sharing the true faith, we will have failed in our ultimate task (2 Timothy 2:1–13).

Based on what you have learned in this lesson, how does the present work of Christ at the right hand of the Father help you to accomplish the Great Commission? Be specific.

How are you involved *personally* in carrying out the work of sharing the faith?

If you feel your involvement in this area is insufficient, what can you do to increase your efforts? Select one or more of the following suggestions, or come up with an idea of your own. Be sure to create a clear plan of how and when you will begin!

__ Invite a non-Christian friend to a movie, sporting event, or other neutral activity to simply foster a friendship. Pray that God would open doors for sharing your faith at the appropriate time.

__ Adopt one of the missionary families your church sponsors, and provide both prayer and financial support.

__ Use your vacation time to take a short-term mission trip, either at home or abroad.

__ Read a book on ministry or missions involvement from those listed in "Resources for Probing Further," section 9, "Works on Ministry and Missions," page 244.

__ Ask your pastor or church leader how you can exercise your spiritual gifts and abilities to help the church further the gospel, and be ready to help out whenever and wherever you're needed.

__ Other: ______________________________

____

____

____

Commit to living out the Great Commission in one of these ways, depending prayerfully on Christ's presence and power through the Holy Spirit to accomplish His will through you.

In this lesson, we learned that the present work of Christ as Mediator, Master, and Friend has very practical—even essential—implications for our present ministry on earth while we await His return. This truth should challenge Christians who are sitting on the sidelines to get into the game! It should also help those who are already involved in ministry to depend on Christ for their strength. He is ready and able to provide all the strength, energy, and courage we need. Only when we're "clothed with power from on high" (Luke 24:49), will we be equipped to lead others on the way of truth in a world of fiction.

Lesson Thirteen

Standing Alone When Outnumbered

Romans 12:1–2; Deuteronomy 6:10–15

THE HEART OF THE MATTER

The Christian life is completely *unlike* the lifestyle of most people on earth. Like tiny islands of truth rooted in an enormous sea of falsehood, Christians live in a world at war with God. The Lord has chosen to leave us in this world, but He does not intend for us to live as though we're the same as the world, as though we belong here. Our situation results in a great dilemma—we often have to stand alone, upholding the way of truth in a world of fiction.

Leader Help

By the end of this lesson, group members should understand the importance of resisting worldly conformity and be ready to embrace spiritual transformation; they should also be emboldened to take a stand for the truth even when outnumbered.

YOU ARE HERE

The following script is a hypothetical dialogue between a modern-day critic of orthodox Christianity and a prepared Christian.

"I just saw the movie *The Da Vinci Code*. It illustrated several issues I've been studying lately. Did you know that Jesus never claimed to be God? In fact, the earliest Christians believed he was just a man—a great rabbi—whose teachings transformed

Leader Help

As with the first hypothetical dialogue you encountered in lesson 2, you may choose to ask two people to read this conversation while others observe or take notes in the margins. Then, work as a group to answer the questions.

their lives. The church didn't start referring to him as God until generations later."

"Yes, I've heard that. It makes for good fiction, but the truth is that Jesus claimed to be God, and His own disciples and Christians since then have understood that He was and is God. The apostle Paul said Jesus created all things and that the fullness of deity dwells in Him in bodily form. And the apostle John specifically addressed this issue at the very beginning of his gospel:, 'In the beginning was the Word, and the Word was with God, and the Word was God. . . . And the Word became flesh, and dwelt among us.'"

"Well, I'll be honest. I've never actually read the whole Bible, but I've read a lot of historical books on the subject and watched some PBS documentaries on the historical Jesus. So I know the books in the Bible were selected from among dozens of competing documents, many of which portrayed Jesus as just a man. You see, *historically* most of the earliest believers thought Jesus was just a great prophet—a man, not God."

"People say many different things about Jesus, but the historical evidence itself is clear. The Christians from the time of the New Testament onward have taught that Jesus is God *and* man, and therefore He is the Lord of all. In fact, one of the earliest false teachings that Christians fought against was Docetism, which taught that Jesus was *only* god and not truly human."

"Well, I read a book by a Harvard scholar—*Harvard*, mind you—saying that the first century of Christian history was characterized by a large group of competing Christianities, with each one claiming to have 'the only truth.' Each of them held to a different view of who Jesus was, and each one provided different 'scriptures' or 'gospels' to support their views. The form of Christianity you're talking about was just one of many, but it eventually won out over all of the other forms. It became the 'Catholic Church' and destroyed its competitors and their 'scriptures.'"

"I've heard that version of history too, but you see, it actually comes from a wrong supposition about who Jesus is. For historians such as these, they don't really care what the evidence is—they interpret it according to their own preconceived biases about Jesus."

"What do you mean?"

"It all boils down to the resurrection of Jesus. *If* Jesus of Nazareth really rose from the dead, then He *is* Lord, whether you believe He is or not. If He rose from the dead, then His disciples really *were* His appointed leaders, salvation really *does* come only through Him, and there really *is* a true view of Jesus and a true view of Scripture. Because the resurrection is the ultimate proof of both His humanity and His deity, if Jesus rose from the dead, then only one view about Him can be correct—*He is Lord*."

"But I don't believe Jesus *literally* rose from the dead. I believe that the resurrection is a myth, a metaphor designed to communicate a deep spiritual truth."

"Historians who don't believe in the bodily resurrection often view the resurrection that way. They have to explain the amazing transformation of the disciples and the explosive growth of the church *somehow*. But the worldview of most of those historians simply doesn't allow for miracles like the resurrection to happen, so they've already concluded that Jesus is not Lord before even looking at the evidence."

"What evidence?"

"If you dig a little deeper, you'll realize you've been reading just one side of the story. Hundreds of books have been written by top-notch scholars who actually *believe* the resurrection of Jesus literally happened—and they provide amazing historical evidence. I'd be glad to give you a book on it if you are interested.'

"Yeah, I'd be interested in looking at it. I try to be open-minded, so I like to hear other points of view."

"That's good to hear. In the end, it all comes down to Jesus—who He is and why He lived—and your decision about Him. It's pretty simple: either He's Lord or He's not. And this decision is worth taking the time to explore. You see, if He hadn't risen from the dead, then I wouldn't waste a second of my life following His teachings. But because He *did* rise from the dead, He's Lord—and we all owe Him our allegiance, no matter what Harvard or Hollywood says about Him . . . even if we have to stand alone in support of that truth."

How did the believer in this dialogue steer the conversation away from the doubter's objections and toward a decision about Jesus Christ? Be specific.

Based on what you learned in previous lessons, what evidence for the truth of Christianity would you suggest to this kind of skeptic? What specific books might you share with him or her?

After completing the lessons in this workbook, do you feel better equipped to take part in a conversation like this one than you did at the beginning of this study? Explain your answer.

____

____

____

____

____

DISCOVERING THE WAY

"Remember the Alamo!"

The siege on the San Antonio mission lasted from February 23 until March 6, 1836. Under General Santa Anna, five thousand Mexican troops surrounded the Alamo and fiercely attacked for thirteen days. Desperately outnumbered, the small group of courageous men inside the Alamo stood alone and fought valiantly. When the battle climaxed with a massive attack over the mission walls, all 182 men inside were killed.

But the war didn't end there. A short time later, a contingent of troops under General Sam Houston mounted a surprise attack at San Jacinto, captured Santa Anna, and secured independence for Texas.

Even though the battle of the Alamo was lost, the war of Texas independence was won—because of a band of dedicated men who were not afraid to stand alone even when outnumbered. Succeeding generations haven't forgotten these valiant men who lost their lives at the Alamo. In fact, the memory of these 182 men became the battle cry for every soldier fighting that war for independence: "Remember the Alamo!"

How is the story of the few brave men who defended the Alamo an apt analogy for the Christian's position in the world?

Even the best analogies usually break down at some point. In light of the principles we've covered in previous lessons, especially in lessons 4 and 12, how might the Alamo illustration fail to accurately represent the believers' relationship to the world?

Standing Alone against the World

Standing alone is never easy. Though we may be set back by minor skirmishes with newscasters and novelists who try to take potshots at the pious or blindside believers, we know that God will ultimately win the spiritual war (Romans 8:31–39). The way of truth will ultimately prevail over the world of fiction.

The fact that Jesus is the risen and ascended Lord of heaven and earth should be enough to convince us to choose His side rather than wander in no-man's land. All the facts we've uncovered and truth we discovered in the previous lessons should move us from the sidelines to join the long line of believers who have taken a stand against the enemies of truth even when outnumbered. In fact, in Romans 12:1–2, Paul urgently pleaded with believers to break away from the instinct to conform that can easily sweep away believers who have failed to take up the baton of the Christian tradition and stand for the center (orthodoxy), the source (Scripture), and the Savior (Jesus Christ).

> The time needs you (as pilots need winds and as a storm-tossed sailor needs a harbor) in order to reach God. . . . Do not let those who appear to be trustworthy yet who teach strange doctrines baffle you. Stand firm, like an anvil being struck with a hammer. It is the mark of a great athlete to be bruised, yet still conquer.[1]
>
> —Ignatius of Antioch (c. AD 110)

Read Paul's address to believers in Romans 12:1–2. What do you see that suggests Paul's request would be difficult to carry out?

List the commands you find in Romans 12:1–2.

According to the last lines of verse 2, what was the intended result of one's obedience to these commands?

Leader Help

If possible, it would be best for the group to use the New American Standard Bible to answer the following questions. This translation is close to the original Greek, and these questions focus on the specific details of the passage.

GETTING TO THE ROOT

The great preacher, Donald Grey Barnhouse, commented on the two key terms in Romans 12:1–2, "conformed" and "transformed."

> The first of these two words, *conformed*, is the translation of a Greek word in the New Testament and it means that we are not to go along with the world's schemes. The second of these words, *transformed*, is a Greek word which means a very radical change from one nature and life to another. It is the word *metamorphoomai* which has given us our word metamorphosis. When a tadpole is changed into a frog or when a grub becomes a butterfly, we speak of it as metamorphosis. There has been a marked and more or less abrupt change in the form and structure of the creature.[2]

For believers, the transformation described in Romans 12:2 isn't cosmetic surgery, it is radical reconstruction—from a human shaped by the world to one who is in the process of being conformed to the image of Christ (Romans 8:29; 1 John 3:2). In other words, consecrating our lives to Christ involves more than simply changing our clothes. It is a radical metamorphosis that begins with presenting yourself to God as a living sacrifice and includes a complete renewal of your mind.

The contours of the world flow along the lines of *fortune*—money and materialism; *fame*—popularity and acceptance; *power*—influence and control; and *pleasure*—sensual desires. In earlier lessons we recognized how heretics in the New Testament and in the early church massaged the unique message of Christianity until it looked more like the world's philosophies and practices and less like the truth of Christ. If our inner convictions are simply lying dormant in a pliable, amorphous mass, we'll be shaped by our peers, the media, and other outside influences rather than being shaped by God. But if we deliberately cultivate biblical convictions and a dynamic personal relationship with Jesus Christ, we will be able to stand strong in the midst of the world's powerful influence.

Read the following passages. Each one warns us regarding the negative influence of the world on believers. When you have finished, write each of these Scriptures as a command.

Psalm 1:1

____

____

____

____

____

Don't become so well-adjusted to your culture that you fit into it without even thinking. Instead, fix your attention on God. You'll be changed from the inside out. Readily recognize what he wants from you, and quickly respond to it. Unlike the culture around you, always dragging you down to its level of immaturity, God brings the best out of you, develops well-formed maturity in you.

(Romans 12:2 MSG)

Proverbs 13:20

Matthew 10:16

John 17:15–16

1 Corinthians 15:33

2 Timothy 4:3–5

Stampeded by the Herd or Standing against the Herd?

If you follow the worldly herd, you'll eventually find yourself caught up in a stampede, running with the crowd at breakneck speed. And if you're not careful, you may just find yourself getting trampled or plunging headlong off the side of a moral cliff. Moses warned the Israelites of just such a danger as they were about to enter the Promised Land, where they would encounter a wild herd of worldly Canaanites.

Read Moses's warning to the Israelites in Deuteronomy 6:10–15. What was the moral trap that endangered the Israelites (6:12)?

Use one or two words to summarize the root cause of this moral failure (6:10–11).

What was the solution to prevent this moral failure (6:12–14)?

Four principles regarding worldly compromise emerge from Deuteronomy 6:10–15. First, getting something for nothing always breeds irresponsibility (6:10–11). Second, this irresponsibility creates a careless attitude (6:12). Third, this attitude leads to a loss of standards (6:13). Finally, this loss prompts insecurity, driving us into the "safety" of conformity to the world's standards (6:14).

The truth is, many Christians today have become too comfortable in their Christianity. They've become irresponsible and careless when it comes to engaging the world in dialogue about the truth of God's Word. Some have slipped into modeling their beliefs and practices after the shallow fiction of the world's system and have turned aside from the way of truth.

How can we keep from forgetting God when the pressures of the world squeeze us tightly? In Deuteronomy 6:4–9, Moses gave the Israelites a string to tie around their spiritual fingers.

Read Deuteronomy 6:4–9. Based on what you've learned through this workbook, summarize this principle in today's terms. How can we love God with all our heart, soul, and might in our current cultural context?

How can we diligently teach the way of truth, not only to our family but also to believers and non-Christians in our spheres of influence? What must you *know* to fulfill this mandate?

What must you *do* to fulfill it?

Leader Help

These questions are intentionally open-ended and recommended for group discussion, drawing on principles from lessons 1 through 12 of this workbook. In order to briefly review those lessons, you might want to consult the "Heart of the Matter" section at the beginning of each lesson and any notes you took throughout the chapter.

STARTING YOUR JOURNEY

Prior to embarking on *The Way of Truth in a World of Fiction*, had you ever seriously considered how the world subtly squeezes you into its mold? The obvious fictions of filmmakers, the documentaries of doubters, and the scholarship of skeptics are just the front-line attacks of the ruler of this age. Yet every day we expose ourselves to Satan's subtle espionage and become the targets of his sinister legion of spiritual assassins. If we are going to be equipped to engage the world of fiction with the way of truth, we must not only be aware of the world's influences, we must also deliberately move to counteract them.

What kinds of friends do you surround yourself with? Are they more "conforming" or "transforming"? Why? How can you tell?

What kinds of books are you reading? What sort of impact might they have on your attitudes, opinions, ideas, and actions?

What kinds of books should you be reading to better prepare yourself to take a stand against the influences of the world?

What kinds of television shows, movies, and music have you watched or listened to most recently? What messages are they communicating? How might they be affecting your thinking?

If any of these personal reflections have pricked your conscience, what do you need to change to bolster your strength to stand against the tides of worldly compromise? Specify at least one action you can take this week. Then do it.

There are two ways of teaching and power, one of light and one of darkness, and there is a great difference between these two ways. For over the one are stationed light-giving angels of God, but over the other are angels of Satan.[3]

—The Epistle of Barnabas (c. AD 100)

Two paths lie before each of us. One is narrow and difficult—the way of truth. The other is broad and easy to walk—the world of fiction.

On the way of truth, the heroes of old engaged in "hand-to-hand" combat with the heretics, standing for the essential truths of the faith. On this path, the Scriptures were preserved, defended, and explained. On this path, Jesus Christ's unique person and work were proclaimed and the Triune God was worshiped and glorified. The way of truth leads to life.

In the world of fiction, however, the truth was maligned and error magnified. The Scriptures were rejected, scoffed at, replaced, added to, or ignored. And Jesus—the God-man who died for the sins of that very same world—was blasphemed, beaten, and crucified, not only by the sinners of the first century but by scholars and critics ever since. The world of fiction leads to death.

Where are you standing today? Are you pursuing the way of truth or dabbling in a world of fiction?

How to Begin a Relationship with God

The world is filled with competing theories about sin and salvation. Alternate views of Jesus vie for our attention at every turn. Different paths to different gods market themselves in the ever-changing desert of ideas. Yet in the midst of this world of contradictory claims, Jesus Christ made a bold assertion: "I am the way, and the truth, and the life; no one comes to the Father but through Me" (John 14:6). In a very real sense, Jesus Himself is *the* Way of Truth in a world of fiction.

Every journey has a beginning, and the way of truth has a first step. Can we be certain we've placed our feet on the right path? The answer to this question comes not from a fly-by-night *New York Times* best-seller but from the all-time best-selling book, translated into more languages and read by more people than any other book in human history. The Bible alone clearly marks the way of truth with four vital markers.

Our Spiritual Condition: Totally Depraved

The first marker is rather personal. One look in the mirror of Scripture, and our human condition becomes painfully clear:

> There is none righteous, not even one;
> There is none who understands,
> There is none who seeks for God;
> All have turned aside, together they have become useless;
> There is none who does good,
> There is not even one. (Romans 3:10–12)

We are all sinners through and through—totally depraved, completely corrupt. Now, that doesn't mean we've committed every atrocity known to humankind. We're not as *bad* as we can be, just as *bad off* as we can be. Sin colors all our thoughts, motives, words, and actions.

You still don't believe it? Look around. Everything in this broken world bears the smudge marks of our sinful nature. Despite our best efforts to create a paradise on earth, crime statistics continue to soar, divorce rates keep climbing, and families keep crumbling.

Something has gone terribly wrong in our society and in ourselves, something deadly. Contrary to how the world would repackage it, "me-first" living doesn't equal rugged individuality and freedom; it equals death. As Paul said in his letter to the Romans, "The wages of sin is death" (Romans 6:23)—our emotional and physical death through sin's destructiveness, and our spiritual death from God's righteous judgment of our sin. This brings us to the second marker: God's character.

God's Character: Infinitely Holy

When he observed the condition of the world and the people in it, the wise King Solomon concluded, "Vanity of vanities, all is vanity" (Ecclesiastes 1:2; 12:8). The fact that we know things are not as they should be points us to a standard of goodness beyond ourselves. Our sense of injustice in life implies a perfect standard of justice. That standard and source is God Himself. And God's standard of holiness contrasts starkly with our sinful condition.

Scripture says that "God is light, and in Him there is no darkness at all" (1 John 1:5). He is absolutely holy—which creates a problem for us. If He is so pure, how can we who are so impure relate to Him?

Perhaps we could try being better people, try to tilt the balance in favor of our good deeds, or seek out wisdom and knowledge for self-improvement. Throughout history, people have attempted to live up to God's standard by keeping the Ten Commandments or by living out their own code of ethics. Unfortunately, no one can come close to satisfying the demands of God's law. Romans 3:20 says, "By the works of the Law no flesh will be justified in His sight; for through the Law comes the knowledge of sin."

Our Need: A Substitute

So here we are, sinners by nature, sinners by choice, trying to pull ourselves up by our own bootstraps and attain a relationship with our holy Creator. But every time we try, we fall flat on our faces. We can't live a good enough life to make up for our sin, because God's standard isn't "good enough"—it's perfection. And we can't make amends for the offense our sin has created without dying for it.

Who can get us out of this mess?

If someone could live perfectly, honoring God's law, and would bear sin's death penalty for us—in our place—then we would be saved from our predicament. But is there such a person? Thankfully, yes!

Meet your substitute—*Jesus Christ*. He is the One who took death's place for you!

> [God] made [Jesus Christ] who knew no sin to be sin on our behalf, so that we might become the righteousness of God in Him. (2 Corinthians 5:21)

God's Provision: A Savior

God rescued us by sending His Son, Jesus, to die on the cross for our sins (1 John 4:9–10). Jesus was fully human and fully divine (John 1:1, 14), a truth that ensures His understanding of our weaknesses, His power to forgive, and His ability to bridge the gap between God and us (Romans 5:6–11). In short, we are "justified as a gift by His grace through the redemption which is in Christ Jesus" (Romans 3:24). Two words in this verse bear further explanation: *justified* and *redemption*.

Justification is God's act of mercy, in which He declares believing sinners righteous, while they are still in their sinning state. Justification doesn't mean that God *makes* us righteous so that we never sin again; rather, He *declares* us righteous—much like a judge pardons a guilty criminal. Because Jesus took our sin upon Himself and suffered our judgment on the cross, God forgives our debt and proclaims us PARDONED.

Redemption is God's act of paying the ransom price to release us from our bondage to sin. Held hostage by Satan, we were shackled by the iron chains of sin and death. Like a loving parent whose child has been kidnapped, God willingly paid the ransom for you. And what a price He paid! He gave His only Son to bear our sins—past, present, and future. Jesus's death and resurrection broke our chains and set us free to become children of God (Romans 6:16–18, 22; Galatians 4:4–7).

Placing Your Faith in Christ

These four markers on the way of truth describe how God has provided a way to Himself through Jesus Christ. Since the price has been paid in full by God, we must respond to His free gift of eternal life in total faith and confidence in Him to save us. We must step forward into the relationship with God that He has prepared for us — not by doing good works or being a good person but by coming to Him just as we are and accepting His justification and redemption by faith.

> For by grace you have been saved through faith; and that not of yourselves, it is the gift of God; not as a result of works, so that no one may boast. (Ephesians 2:8–9)

We accept God's gift of salvation simply by placing our faith in Christ alone for the forgiveness of our sins. Would you like to enter a relationship with your Creator by trusting in Christ as your Savior? If so, here's a simple prayer you can use to express your faith:

> *Dear God,*
>
> *I know that my sin has put a barrier between You and me. Thank You for sending Your Son, Jesus, to die in my place. I trust in Jesus alone to forgive my sins, and I accept His gift of eternal life. I ask Jesus to be my personal Savior and the Lord of my life. Thank You. In Jesus's name, amen.*

If you've prayed this prayer or one like it and you wish to find out more about knowing God and His plan for you in the Bible, contact us at Insight for Living. You can speak to one of our pastors on staff by calling 972-473-5097. Or you can write to us at the address below.

Of all the relationships you enjoy in this life, none can compare with a relationship with God through Jesus Christ, who loved us and gave Himself for us. That first step by faith onto the way of truth begins a personal and eternal relationship with God.

> Pastoral Ministries Department
> Insight for Living
> Post Office Box 269000
> Plano, Texas 75026-9000

Endnotes

Lesson 1

Unless otherwise noted below, all material in this chapter is based on or quoted from "An Exposé of Counterfeit Communicators," a sermon by Charles R. Swindoll and supplemented by the Creative Ministries department of Insight for Living.

1. Christopher Edwards, *Crazy for God* (Englewood Cliffs, N.J.: Prentice-Hall, 1979), foreword.

2. Irenaeus, *Against Heresies* 1.1.2. In *The Ante-Nicene Fathers: Translations of the Writings of the Fathers down to AD 325*, ed. Alexander Roberts, James Donaldson, and A. Cleveland Coxe, vol. 1, *The Apostolic Fathers, Justin Martyr, Irenaeus*, American reprint ed. (New York: Charles Scribner's Sons, 1899), 315.

3. Walter Bauer and others, eds., *A Greek-English Lexicon of the New Testament and Other Early Christian Literature*, 2d rev. ed. (Chicago: University of Chicago Press, 1979), 23–24.

4. Walter Bauer and others, *A Greek-English Lexicon*, 666.

Lesson 2

Unless otherwise noted below, all material in this chapter is based on or quoted from "The Acts of the Apostates," a sermon by Charles R. Swindoll and supplemented by the Creative Ministries department of Insight for Living.

1. Ignatius, *Letter to the Magnesians* 11. In *The Apostolic Fathers: Greek Texts and English Translations*, updated ed., ed. and rev. Michael W. Holmes, ed. and trans. J. B. Lightfoot and J. R. Harmer (Grand Rapids: Baker Books, 1999), 157. Used by permission of Baker Academic, a division of Baker Publishing.

2. "The Nicene Creed," in *The Hymnal for Worship and Celebration*, ed. Tom Fettke and Ken Barker (Waco, Tex.: Word Music, 1986), no. 717.

3. Fritz Rienecker, *A Linguistic Key to the Greek New Testament*, trans. and ed. by Cleon L. Rogers, Jr. (Grand Rapids: Zondervan, 1980), 803.

4. "The Nicene Creed," in *The Hymnal for Worship and Celebration*, ed. Tom Fettke and Ken Barker (Waco, Tex.: Word Music, 1986), no. 717.

5. "The Apostles Creed," in *The Hymnal for Worship and Celebration*, ed. Tom Fettke and Ken Barker (Waco, Tex.: Word Music, 1986), no. 716.

Lesson 3

Unless otherwise noted below, all material in this chapter is based on or quoted from "Why Bother to Battle?" a sermon by Charles R. Swindoll and supplemented by the Creative Ministries department of Insight for Living.

1. Millard J. Erickson, *Christian Theology*, 2d. ed. (Grand Rapids: Baker Books, 1998), 1197.

2. Michael Green, *The Second Epistle General of Peter and the General Epistle of Jude: An Introduction and Commentary*, The Tyndale New Testament Commentaries Series (Grand Rapids: Wm. B. Eerdmans, 1968), 181.

3. *Didache* 1.1. In *The Apostolic Fathers: Greek Texts and English Translations*, updated ed., ed. and rev. Michael W. Holmes, ed. and trans. J. B. Lightfoot and J. R. Harmer (Grand Rapids: Baker Books, 1999), 251. Used by permission of Baker Academic, a division of Baker Publishing.

4. *Martyrdom of Polycarp* 9.3–10.1. In *The Apostolic Fathers: Greek Texts and English Translations*, updated ed., ed. and rev. Michael W. Holmes, ed. and trans. J. B. Lightfoot and J. R. Harmer (Grand Rapids: Baker Books, 1999), 235.

Lesson 4

Unless otherwise noted below, all material in this chapter is based on or quoted from "Get Your Act Together!" a sermon by Charles R. Swindoll and supplemented by the Creative Ministries department of Insight for Living.

1. Sir Winston Churchill, as quoted in *Bartlett's Familiar Quotations*, 16th ed., ed. Justin Kaplan (Boston: Little, Brown, 1992), 620.

2. Polycarp, *To the Philippians* 7.2. In *The Apostolic Fathers: Greek Texts and English Translations*, updated ed., ed. and rev. Michael W. Holmes, ed. and trans. J. B. Lightfoot and J. R. Harmer (Grand Rapids: Baker Books, 1999), 215. Used by permission of Baker Academic, a division of Baker Publishing.

3. Some examples of these scholars are Bart D. Ehrman, Elaine Pagels, Karen King, John Dominic Crossan, John Shelby Spong, and Robert Funk.

4. For a thorough and accessible treatment of orthodoxy and heresy in early Christianity, see Darrell L. Bock, *The Missing Gospels: Unearthing the Truth about Alternative Christianities* (Nashville: Nelson Books, 2006).

5. Irenaeus, *Against Heresies* 3.2.3. In *The Ante-Nicene Fathers: Translations of the Writings of the Fathers down to* AD *325*, ed. Alexander Roberts, James Donaldson, and A. Cleveland Coxe, vol. 1, *The Apostolic Fathers, Justin Martyr, Irenaeus*, American reprint ed. (New York: Charles Scribner's Sons, 1899), 415.

Lesson 5

Unless otherwise noted below, all material in this chapter is based on or quoted from "One Library of Living Truth," a sermon by Charles R. Swindoll and supplemented by the Creative Ministries department of Insight for Living.

1. Bernard Ramm, *Protestant Christian Evidences* (Chicago: Moody, 1966), 232.

2. Walter Bauer and others, eds., *A Greek-English Lexicon of the New Testament and Other Early Christian Literature*, 2d rev. ed. (Chicago: University of Chicago Press, 1979), 141.

3. See Roland K. Harrison, "Bible," in *The International Standard Bible Encyclopedia*, vol. 1, *A–D*, rev. ed., ed. Geoffrey W. Bromiley and others (Grand Rapids: Wm. B. Eerdmans, 1988), 482–483.

4. For a history of doctrinal authority during the development of the New Testament, see Darrell L. Bock, *The Missing Gospels: Unearthing the Truth about Alternative Christianities* (Nashville: Nelson Books, 2006).

5. For thorough treatments of the issue of canonicity of Old and New Testament books, see F. F. Bruce, *The Canon of Scripture* (Downers Grove, Ill.: InterVarsity, 1988); Bruce M. Metzger, *The Canon of the New Testament: Its Origin, Development, and Significance* (Oxford: Clarendon, 1987); Robert P. Meye, "The Canon of the NT," in *The International Standard Bible Encyclopedia*, vol. 1, *A–D*, ed. Geoffrey W. Bromiley (Grand Rapids: Wm. B. Eerdmans, 1988), 601–606.

6. Ignatius, *To the Philadelphians* 9.2. In *The Apostolic Fathers: Greek Texts and English Translations*, updated ed., ed. and rev. Michael W. Holmes, ed. and trans. J. B. Lightfoot and J. R. Harmer (Grand Rapids: Baker Books, 1999), 183. Used by permission of Baker Academic, a division of Baker Publishing.

7. Irenaeus, *Against Heresies* 2.27.2. In *The Ante-Nicene Fathers: Translations of the Writings of the Fathers down to* AD *325*, ed. Alexander Roberts, James Donaldson, and A. Cleveland Coxe, vol. 1, *The Apostolic Fathers, Justin Martyr, Irenaeus*, American reprint ed. (New York: Charles Scribner's Sons, 1899), 398.

Lesson 6

Unless otherwise noted below, all material in this chapter is based on or quoted from "Be Sure of Your Source," a sermon by Charles R. Swindoll and supplemented by the Creative Ministries department of Insight for Living.

1. Josh McDowell and Bob Hostetler, *Right from Wrong: What You Need to Know to Help Youth Make Right Choices* (Dallas: Word, 1994), 13.

2. *1 Clement* 45.2–3. In *The Apostolic Fathers: Greek Texts and English Translations,* updated ed., ed. and rev. Michael W. Holmes, ed. and trans. J. B. Lightfoot and J. R. Harmer (Grand Rapids: Baker Books, 1999), 79. Used by permission of Baker Academic, a division of Baker Publishing.

3. Charles C. Ryrie, *Basic Theology* (Wheaton, Ill.: SP Publications, Victor Books, 1986), 71.

4. An excellent resource for those interested in the reasoning behind certain English translations is the *Net Bible*, available online at www.netbible.org.

5. Kenneth O. Gangel, "2 Peter," in *The Bible Knowledge Commentary*, New Testament ed., ed. John F. Walvoord and Roy B. Zuck (Wheaton, Ill.: SP Publications, Victor Books, 1988), 869.

6. Gangel, "2 Peter," in *The Bible Knowledge Commentary*, 869.

7. Examples of these claims abound. Some of the more popular come from authors like Bart Ehrman, Elaine Pagels, John Shelby Spong, and John Dominic Crossan.

Lesson 7

Unless otherwise noted below, all material in this chapter is based on or quoted from "Jesus: His Existence before Creation," a sermon by Charles R. Swindoll and supplemented by the Creative Ministries department of Insight for Living.

1. Excerpt from *Surprised by Joy: The Shape of My Early Life* by C. S. Lewis, copyright © 1956 by C. S. Lewis and renewed 1984 by Arthur Owen Barfield, reprinted by permission of Harcourt, Inc.
   For distribution in English throughout the British Commonwealth: *Surprised by Joy* by C. S. Lewis, copyright © 1955 by C. S. Lewis Pte. Ltd. Extract reprinted by permission.

2. C. S. Lewis, *Mere Christianity*, rev. and enlarged ed. (New York: Macmillan, 1952), 55–57.

3. *Epistle to Diognetus* 11.4–5. In *The Apostolic Fathers: Greek Texts and English Translations*, updated ed., ed. and rev. Michael W. Holmes, ed. and trans. J. B. Lightfoot and J. R. Harmer (Grand Rapids: Baker Books, 1999), 551. Used by permission of Baker Academic, a division of Baker Publishing.

4. Some, like Jehovah's Witnesses, have tried to get around Thomas's confession of Jesus as God by saying that Thomas was speaking to Christ when he said "My Lord" but speaking to the Father when he said "My God!" However, the Greek text clearly says that Thomas said these things "to Him" (*autō*) in both cases. Also, notice that Jesus did not rebuke Thomas for calling Him "God."

5. Ignatius, *Letter to the Ephesians* 7.2. In *The Apostolic Fathers: Greek Texts and English Translations*, updated ed., ed. and rev. Michael W. Holmes, ed. and trans. J. B. Lightfoot and J. R. Harmer (Grand Rapids: Baker Books, 1999), 141.

6. *The Martyrdom of Polycarp* 14.3. In *The Apostolic Fathers: Greek Texts and English Translations*, updated ed., ed. and rev. Michael W. Holmes, ed. and trans. J. B. Lightfoot and J. R. Harmer (Grand Rapids: Baker Books, 1999), 239.

Lesson 8

Unless otherwise noted below, all material in this chapter is based on or quoted from "Jesus: A Birth like None Other," a sermon by Charles R. Swindoll and supplemented by the Creative Ministries department of Insight for Living.

1. Ignatius, *Letter to the Ephesians* 19.1, 3. In *The Apostolic Fathers: Greek Texts and English Translations*, updated ed., ed. and rev. Michael W. Holmes, ed. and trans. J. B. Lightfoot and J. R. Harmer (Grand Rapids: Baker Books, 1999), 149. Used by permission of Baker Academic, a division of Baker Publishing.

2. Francis Brown, S. R. Driver, and Charles A. Briggs, *The Brown-Driver-Briggs Hebrew and English Lexicon* (Boston: Houghton, Mifflin, 1906; reprint, Peabody, Mass.: Hendrickson, 1996), 761.

3. Walter Bauer and other, eds., *A Greek-English Lexicon of the New Testament and Other Early Christian Literature*, 2d rev. ed. (Chicago: University of Chicago Press, 1979), 627.

4. Melito, *On Pascha* 8. In Alistair Stewart-Sykes, *Melito of Sardis, On Pascha, with the Fragments of Melito and Other Material Related to the Quartodecimans* (Crestwood, N.Y.: St. Vladimir's Seminary Press, 2001), 39.

Lesson 9

Unless otherwise noted below, all material in this chapter is based on or quoted from "Jesus: His God-Man Lifestyle," a sermon by Charles R. Swindoll and supplemented by the Creative Ministries department of Insight for Living

1. Norman P. Tanner, ed., *Decrees of the Ecumenical Councils*, vol. 1, *Nicaea I to Lateran V*, 86. Copyright © 1990 by Sheed & Ward and Georgetown University Press. Reprinted by permission of the publisher.

2. For a history of creeds, see A. S. Wood, "Creeds and Confessions," in *The International Standard Bible Encyclopedia,* vol. 1, *A–D*, rev. ed., ed. Geoffrey W. Bromiley and others (Grand Rapids: Wm. B. Eerdmans, 1979), 805–812.

3. Translated from the Greek by Michael J. Svigel from the text in Tanner, ed., *Decrees of the Ecumenical Councils*, 86.

4. Tanner, ed., *Decrees of the Ecumenical Councils*, 86.

5. For further background on the issue of Jesus and Mary Magdalene, see Darrell L. Bock, *Breaking the Da Vinci Code: Answers to the Questions Everyone's Asking* (Nashville: Nelson Books, 2004), 31–59; and Erwin W. Lutzer, *The Da Vinci Deception* (Wheaton, Ill.: Tyndale House, 2004), 39–57.

6. Tanner, ed., *Decrees of the Ecumenical Councils*, 86–87.

Lesson 10

Unless otherwise noted below, all material in this chapter is based on or quoted from "Jesus: A Lamb Led to Slaughter," a sermon by Charles R. Swindoll and supplemented by the Creative Ministries department of Insight for Living.

1. Max Lucado, *No Wonder They Call Him the Savior* (Portland, Ore.: Multnomah, 1986), 57–58.

2. Justin Martyr, *First Apology* 13. In Alexander Roberts and James Donaldson, eds., *The Ante-Nicene Fathers*, vol. 1, *The Apostolic Fathers, Justin Martyr, Irenaeus*, American reprint ed. (New York: Charles Scribner's Sons, 1899), 166–167.

3. Robert Letham, *The Work of Christ*, Contours of Christian Theology, ed. Gerald Bray (Downers Grove, Ill.: InterVarsity, 1993), 139.

4. For discussions on the nature and effects of the atonement, see Robert Letham, *The Work of Christ*, 125–157; and Earl D. Radmacher, "Salvation: A Necessary Work of God," in Charles R. Swindoll and Roy B. Zuck, eds., *Understanding Christian Theology* (Nashville: Thomas Nelson, 2003), 832–837.

5. Irenaeus, *Against Heresies* 5.1.1. In Alexander Roberts and James Donaldson, eds., *The Ante-Nicene Fathers*, vol. 1, *The Apostolic Fathers, Justin Martyr, Irenaeus* (New York: Charles Scribner's Sons, 1899), 527.

Lesson 11

Unless otherwise noted below, all material in this chapter is based on or quoted from "Jesus: Triumphant over the Grave," a sermon by Charles R. Swindoll and supplemented by the Creative Ministries department of Insight for Living.

1. Irenaeus, *Against Heresies* 1.24.4. In *The Ante-Nicene Fathers: Translations of the Writings of the Fathers down to AD 325*, ed. Alexander Roberts, James Donaldson, and A. Cleveland Coxe, vol. 1, *The Apostolic Fathers, Justin Martyr, Irenaeus*, American reprint ed. (New York: Charles Scribner's Sons, 1899) 349.

2. *1 Clement* 42.3. In *The Apostolic Fathers: Greek Texts and English Translations*, updated ed., ed. and rev. Michael W. Holmes, ed. and trans. J. B. Lightfoot and J. R. Harmer (Grand Rapids: Baker Books, 1999), 75. Used by permission of Baker Academic, a division of Baker Publishing.

3. Ignatius, *Letter to the Smyrnaeans* 3.1–2. In *The Apostolic Fathers: Greek Texts and English Translations*, updated ed., ed. and rev. Michael W. Holmes, ed. and trans. J. B. Lightfoot and J. R. Harmer (Grand Rapids: Baker Books, 1999), 187.

4. *1 Clement* 5.6–7. In *The Apostolic Fathers: Greek Texts and English Translations*, updated ed., ed. and rev. Michael W. Holmes, ed. and trans. J. B. Lightfoot and J. R. Harmer (Grand Rapids: Baker Books, 1999), 35.

Lesson 12

Unless otherwise noted below, all material in this chapter is based on or quoted from "Jesus: Ascended and Seated in Heaven," a sermon by Charles R. Swindoll and supplemented by the Creative Ministries department of Insight for Living.

1. Justin Martyr, *Dialogue with Trypho* 39. In *The Ante-Nicene Fathers: Translations of the Writings of the Fathers down to AD 325*, ed. Alexander Roberts, James Donaldson, and A. Cleveland Coxe, vol. 1, *The Apostolic Fathers, Justin Martyr, Irenaeus*, American reprint ed. (New York: Charles Scribner's Sons, 1899), 214.

2. Some of the more radical expressions of this theory today are from popular historians such as Bart Ehrman and Elaine Pagels.

3. Irenaeus, *Against Heresies* 1.10.1, 2. In *The Ante-Nicene Fathers: Translations of the Writings of the Fathers down to* AD *325*, ed. Alexander Roberts, James Donaldson, and A. Cleveland Coxe, vol. 1, *The Apostolic Fathers, Justin Martyr, Irenaeus*, American reprint ed. (New York: Charles Scribner's Sons, 1899), 330–331.

4. For an evangelical account of how the Christian faith was preserved and passed down during the earliest years of Christianity, see Darrell L. Bock, *The Missing Gospels: Unearthing the Truth about Alternative Christianities* (Nashville: Nelson Books, 2006).

5. Irenaeus, *Fragment* 54. In *The Ante-Nicene Fathers: Translations of the Writings of the Fathers down to* AD *325*, ed. Alexander Roberts, James Donaldson, and A. Cleveland Coxe, vol. 1, *The Apostolic Fathers, Justin Martyr, Irenaeus*, American reprint ed. (New York: Charles Scribner's Sons, 1899), 577.

Lesson 13

Unless otherwise noted below, all material in this chapter is based on or quoted from "Standing Alone When Outnumbered," a sermon by Charles R. Swindoll and supplemented by the Creative Ministries department of Insight for Living.

1. Ignatius, *Letter to Polycarp* 2.3, 3.1. In *The Apostolic Fathers: Greek Texts and English Translations*, updated ed., ed. and rev. Michael W. Holmes, ed. and trans. J. B. Lightfoot and J. R. Harmer (Grand Rapids: Baker Books, 1999), 197. Used by permission of Baker Academic, a division of Baker Publishing.

2. Donald Grey Barnhouse, "God's Discipline" in *Expositions of Bible Doctrines Taking the Epistle to the Romans as a Point of Departure*, vol. 4 (1964; repr., Grand Rapids: Wm. B. Eerdmans, 1988), 27.

3. *The Epistle of Barnabas* 18.1. In *The Apostolic Fathers: Greek Texts and English Translations*, updated ed., ed. and rev. Michael W. Holmes, ed. and trans. J. B. Lightfoot and J. R. Harmer (Grand Rapids: Baker Books, 1999), 321.

Resources for Probing Further

Some of the issues addressed in this workbook could take a lifetime to explore, and we were able to introduce them only briefly. However, we would like to suggest the following resources for digging deeper into these important topics. Most of these books should be available either in your church or public library, bookstore, or online booksellers, though some may be out of print. Several can be purchased through the Insight for Living Web site at **www.insight.org**.

Of course, we cannot always endorse everything a writer says, and we encourage you to approach these and all other extra-biblical resources with wisdom and discernment. However, for their particular area of study, these are some of the best resources, and their strengths outweigh any weaknesses.

To help you decide which resources are best for you, we've categorized the books as "beginner," "intermediate," "advanced," or "expert."

Section 1
For Specific Challenges Made by *The Da Vinci Code* Novel or Film

Bock, Darrell L. *Breaking the Da Vinci Code: Answers to the Questions Everyone's Asking*. Nashville: Nelson Books, 2004. (beginner/intermediate)

Lutzer, Erwin W. *The Da Vinci Deception*. Wheaton, Ill.: Tyndale House, 2004. (beginner)

Witherington III, Ben. *The Gospel Code: Novel Claims about Jesus, Mary Magdalene and Da Vinci*. Downers Grove, Ill.: InterVarsity, 2004. (beginner/intermediate)

Section 2
General Works on Christian Theology and Doctrine

Bible.org. This evangelical Web site hosts not only the *Net Bible* but also countless articles on biblical studies as well as theological and current topics. Access is free at www.bible.org. (beginner/intermediate/advanced/expert)

Erickson, Millard J. *Christian Theology*. 2d. ed. Grand Rapids: Baker Books, 1998. (advanced)

Little, Paul E. *Know What You Believe*. Revised and expanded ed. Colorado Springs: Chariot Victor, 1999. (beginner)

Ryrie, Charles C. *Basic Theology: A Popular Systematic Guide to Understanding Biblical Truth*. Chicago: Moody, 1999. (intermediate)

Stott, John R. W. *Basic Christianity*. Rev. ed. Grand Rapids: Wm. B. Eerdmans, 1981. (intermediate)

Swindoll, Charles R., *Growing Deep in the Christian Life: Essential Truths for Becoming Strong in the Faith*. Grand Rapids: Zondervan, 1995. (beginner)

Swindoll, Charles R. and Roy B. Zuck, eds. *Understanding Christian Theology*. Nashville: Thomas Nelson, 2003. (intermediate)

Section 3
Defenses of the Christian Faith (Apologetics)

Craig, William Lane. *Reasonable Faith: Christian Truth and Apologetics*. Revised ed. Wheaton, Ill.: Crossway Books, 1994. (beginner/intermediate)

Geisler, Norman L., and Thomas Howe. *When Critics Ask: A Popular Handbook on Bible Difficulties*. Grand Rapids: Baker Books, 1997. (beginner/intermediate)

Geisler, Norman L., and Ronald M. Brooks. *When Skeptics Ask: A Handbook of Christian Evidences*. Grand Rapids: Wheaton, Ill.: Victor Books, 1990. (beginner/intermediate)

Little, Paul E. *Know Why You Believe*. Revised and expanded ed. Downers Grove, Ill.: InterVarsity, 2000. (beginner)

McDowell, Josh. *More Than a Carpenter*. Wheaton, Ill.: Tyndale House, 1977. (beginner)

______. *The New Evidence That Demands a Verdict*. Revised and expanded ed. Nashville: Thomas Nelson, 1999. (intermediate)

Nash, Ronald H. *Faith and Reason: Searching for a Rational Faith*. Grand Rapids: Academie Books, 1988. (intermediate)

Strobel, Lee. *The Case for Christ: A Journalist's Personal Investigation of the Evidence for Jesus*. Grand Rapids: Zondervan, 1998. (beginner/intermediate)

Section 4
Works on the History of the Church, Including the Earliest Centuries

Bingham, D. Jeffrey. *Pocket History of the Church*. Downers Grove, Ill.: InterVarsity, 2002. (intermediate)

Bock, Darrell L. *The Missing Gospels: Unearthing the Truth about Alternative Christianities*. Nashville: Nelson Books, 2006. (intermediate)

Frend, W. H. C. *The Rise of Christianity*. Minneapolis: Fortress, 1984. (advanced)

González, Justo L. *The Story of Christianity: The Early Church to the Dawn of the Reformation*. Vol. 1. San Francisco: HarperSanFrancisco, 1984. (intermediate/advanced)

______. *The Story of Christianity: The Reformation to the Present Day*. Vol. 2. San Francisco: HarperSanFrancisco, 1985. (intermediate/advanced)

Guy, Laurie. *Introducing Early Christianity: A Topical Survey of Its Life, Beliefs and Practices*. Downers Grove, Ill.: InterVarsity, 2004. (intermediate/advanced)

Komoszewski, J. Ed, M. James Sawyer, and Daniel B. Wallace. *Reinventing Jesus: What* The Da Vinci Code *and Other Novel Speculations Don't Tell You*. Grand Rapids: Kregel, 2006. (intermediate)

Robinson, Thomas A. *The Bauer Thesis Examined: The Geography of Heresy in the Early Christian Church*. Studies in the Bible and Early Christianity 11. Lewiston, N.Y.: Edwin Mellen, 1988. (expert)

Shelley, Bruce L. *Church History in Plain Language*. Updated 2nd ed. Waco, Tex.: Word, 1995. (beginner/intermediate)

Skarsaune, Oskar. *In the Shadow of the Temple: Jewish Influences on Early Christianity*. Downers Grove, Ill.: InterVarsity, 2002. (intermediate/advanced)

Turner, H. E. W. *The Pattern of Christian Truth: A Study in the Relations between Orthodoxy and Heresy in the Early Church*. London: Mowbray, 1954. (expert)

Section 5
Primary Texts by the Early Church Fathers and Heretical Groups

The Apostolic Fathers: Greek Texts and English Translations. Updated ed. Ed. and rev. Michael W. Holmes, ed. and trans. J. B. Lightfoot and J. R. Harmer. Grand Rapids: Baker Books, 1999. (NOTE: English-only edition is also available.) (intermediate/advanced)

The Ante-Nicene Fathers: Translations of the Writings of the Fathers down to AD *325*. Ed. Alexander Roberts, James Donaldson, and A. Cleveland Coxe. Vol. 1, *The Apostolic Fathers, Justin Martyr, Irenaeus*. American reprint ed. New York: Charles Scribner's Sons, 1899. (intermediate/advanced)

Christian Classics Ethereal Library. This is an online collection of historical Christian writings in the public domain. Access is free, and their collection is quite extensive. These can be accessed at www.ccel.org. (intermediate/advanced)

Robinson, James M., ed. *The Nag Hammadi Library in English*. Trans. Coptic Gnostic Library Project. 1st U.S. ed. New York: Harper and Row, 1977. (advanced/expert)

Stewart-Sykes, Alistair. *Melito of Sardis, On Pascha, with the Fragments of Melito and Other Material Related to the Quartodecimans*. Crestwood, N.Y.: St. Vladimir's Seminary Press, 2001. (intermediate/advanced)

Section 6
Works on the Origins and Reliability of Scripture

Beckwith, Roger T. *The Old Testament Canon of the New Testament Church and its Background in Early Judaism*. Grand Rapids: Wm. B. Eerdmans, 1986. (intermediate)

Bruce, F. F. *The Canon of Scripture*. Downers Grove, Ill.: InterVarsity, 1988. (intermediate)

Geisler, Norman. *Inerrancy*. Grand Rapids: Zondervan, 1980. (intermediate)

Lutzer, Erwin W. *Seven Reasons Why You Can Trust the Bible*. Chicago: Moody, 1998. (beginner)

Metzger, Bruce M. *The Canon of the New Testament: Its Origin, Development, and Significance*. Oxford: Clarendon, 1987. (advanced/expert)

Section 7
Biblical, Historical, and Theological Treatments of Christ's Person and Work

Erickson, Millard J. *The Word Became Flesh: A Contemporary Incarnational Christology*. Grand Rapids: Baker Books, 1991. (advanced)

Harris, Murray J. *Three Crucial Questions about Jesus*. Grand Rapids: Baker Books, 1994. (intermediate)

———. *Jesus as God: The New Testament Use of Theos in Reference to Jesus*. Grand Rapids: Baker Books, 1992. (advanced/expert)

Hurtado, Larry W. *Lord Jesus Christ: Devotion to Jesus in Earliest Christianity*. Grand Rapids: Wm. B. Eerdmans, 2003. (advanced/expert)

Letham, Robert. *The Work of Christ*. Contours of Christian Theology, ed. Gerald Bray. Downers Grove, Ill.: InterVarsity, 1993. (intermediate/advanced)

Section 8
Works on the Resurrection of Jesus Christ

Craig, William Lane, Paul Copan, and Ronald K. Tacelli, eds. *Jesus' Resurrection: Fact or Figment? A Debate Between William Lane Craig and Gerd Lüdemann*. Downers Grove, Ill.: InterVarsity, 2000. (intermediate/advanced)

Habermas, Gary R. and Michael R. Licona. *The Case for the Resurrection of Jesus*. Grand Rapids: Kregel, 2004. (intermediate)

McDowell, Josh. *The Resurrection Factor*. San Bernardino, Cal.: Here's Life Publishers, 1981 (beginner)

Strobel, Lee. *The Case for Easter: A Journalist Investigates the Evidence for the Resurrection*. Grand Rapids: Zondervan, 2003. (beginner)

Wright, N. T. *The Resurrection of the Son of God*. Christian Origins and the Question of God. London: SPCK, 2003. (expert)

Section 9
Works on Ministry and Missions

Bennett, Rob and John Purvis. *The Adventure of Discipling Others: Training in the Art of Disciplemaking*. Colorado Springs: NavPress, 2003. (intermediate)

Cecil, Douglas M. *The 7 Principles of an Evangelistic Life*. Chicago: Moody, 2003. (beginner/intermediate)

Hendricks, Howard. *As Iron Sharpens Iron: Building Character in a Mentoring Relationship*. Chicago: Moody, 2000. (beginner/intermediate)

Henrichsen, Walter A. *Disciples Are Made, Not Born: How to Help Others Grow to Maturity in Christ*. Colorado Springs: Victor, Cook Communications, 1988. (beginner/intermediate)

Insight for Living. *Creating a Legacy Workbook*. Plano, Tex.: IFL Publishing House, 2005. (beginner)

Malphurs, Aubrey. *Maximizing Your Effectiveness: How to Discover and Develop Your Divine Design*. Grand Rapids: Baker Books, 1995. (intermediate)

Ordering Information

The Way of Truth in a World of Fiction

If you would like to order additional workbooks, purchase the audio series that accompanies this workbook, or request our product catalog, please contact the office that serves you.

United States and International Locations

Insight for Living
Post Office Box 269000
Plano, Texas 75026-9000
1-800-772-8888, 24 hours a day, seven days a week (U.S. contacts)
International constituents may contact the U.S. office through mail queries or call 972-473-5136.
www.insight.org

Canada

Insight for Living Ministries
Post Office Box 2510
Vancouver, BC V6B 3W7
1-800-663-7639
www.insightforliving.ca

Australia and South Pacific

Insight for Living, Inc.
Post Office Box 1011
Bayswater, VIC 3153
AUSTRALIA
1300 467 444
www.insight.asn.au